Elite • 174

American Civil War Guerrilla Tactics

SEAN McLACHLAN

ILLUSTRATED BY G & S EMBLETON

Consultant editor Martin Windrow

First published in Great Britain in 2009 by Osprey Publishing,
Midland House, West Way, Botley, Oxford OX2 0PH, UK
443 Park Avenue South, New York, NY 10016, USA
Email: info@ospreypublishing.com

ISBN: 978 184603 494 7
ebook ISBN: 978 1 84908 108 5

Editor: Martin Windrow
Design: Ken Vail Graphic Design, Cambridge, UK (kvgd.com)
Typeset in Sabon and Myriad Pro
Index by Fineline Editorial Services
Originated by PPS Grasmere, Leeds, UK
Printed in China through World Print Ltd.

09 10 11 12 13   9 8 7 6 5 4 3 2 1

A CIP catalogue record for this book is available from the British Library

FOR A CATALOGUE OF ALL BOOKS PUBLISHED BY OSPREY MILITARY
AND AVIATION PLEASE CONTACT:

Osprey Direct, c/o Random House Distribution Center,
400 Hahn Road, Westminster, MD 21157
Email: uscustomerservice@ospreypublishing.com

Osprey Direct, The Book Service Ltd, Distribution Centre,
Colchester Road, Frating Green, Colchester, Essex, CO7 7DW
E-mail: customerservice@ospreypublishing.com

www.ospreypublishing.com

DEDICATION

This book is dedicated to Almudena, my wife, and Julián, my son

ACKNOWLEDGEMENTS

The author wishes to thank the following for their generous assistance:

Rex Dixon and Caitlin Lenon for their hospitality; the Kneighborhood
Knights for chess and conversation; Ed Bailey for recounting his experience
firing black powder weapons; the staffs of the State Historical Society of
Missouri, Kansas State Historical Society, and Littlejohn Collection for their
help in finding photos and primary documents; and Dawn Andrus and
Robert Feeney for details on Civil War wiretapping.

All photos credited (LoC) are courtesy of the Library of Congress, Photo
and Print Division.

ARTIST'S NOTE

Readers may care to note that the original paintings from which the
colour plates in this book were prepared are available for private sale.
All reproduction copyright whatsoever is retained by the Publishers.
All enquiries should be addressed to:

www.gerryembleton.com

The Publishers regret that they can enter into no correspondence
upon this matter.

THE WOODLAND TRUST

Osprey Publishing are supporting the Woodland Trust, the UK's leading
woodland conservation charity, by funding the dedication of trees.

CONTENTS

AMERICAN CIVIL WAR GUERRILLA TACTICS

INTRODUCTION

At the beginning of the American Civil War in 1861 the Confederacy faced serious strategic problems. The North had a greater landmass, a larger population, more industry, more railroads, and more munitions factories. The populations in Border States such as Missouri, Tennessee, Kentucky, and Virginia had divided loyalties, and even in the deepest South there were "Tories" who wanted to remain in the Union. Every single state in the Confederacy contributed troops to the Union army. Given this situation, it is no surprise that in the Border States an extensive and bitter guerrilla war between Unionists and Secessionists paralleled – and indeed anticipated – the major operations of the regular armies, while Southern Tories fought to keep the flame of Unionism alive far from the battlefront. Americans had a deep-rooted tradition of hit-and-run irregular warfare stretching back long before the American Revolution, and the independent spirit and distrust of authority that typifies American culture prompted many individuals to fight for their cause outside the ranks of regular armies.

Quantrill's attack on Lawrence, Kansas, on August 21, 1863 horrified Northerners and many Southerners. This abolitionist town had already been looted by Missourians in May 1856, but in 1863 Quantrill's guerrillas virtually destroyed it, killing nearly 200 men and boys. While on this occasion the Southern ethos of chivalry prevented them from directly harming women, such restraint was far from universal among irregular fighters. (LoC)

"Bleeding Kansas": a band of Missouri "border ruffians" depicted in a Northern publication as drunk, disorderly, and armed. This is no exaggeration, but the Kansans who raided Missouri farms were no better. (Kansas State Historical Society)

Some definition of terms is immediately necessary. "Guerrilla" has been used to describe a wide range of warriors both then and since; in this book the term refers to those fighters on either side who did not join (or had deserted from) the regular army, yet continued to fight. "Bushwhackers" refers to Rebel guerrillas in Missouri, who acted somewhat differently to their comrades in other states. "Jayhawkers" denotes their Unionist counterparts in Kansas. "Partisan rangers" were distinct from guerrillas in that they enjoyed some level of recognition from the army or government. In the case of Southern partisan rangers, they might have been organized under the Partisan Ranger Act of 1862, or by one of the state governments; the Union passed no such act, but the US Army and sometimes even the Federal government recognized independent units.

A third type of fighter, the cavalry raider, fits into the definition of irregular warfare only by virtue of his tactics. Some, such as Nathan Bedford Forrest and John Hunt Morgan, occasionally acted as partisans while actually being part of the Confederate Army. Union commanders and later historians often referred to these two famous generals as guerrillas or partisans, but in fact they were regular soldiers using irregular tactics.

All three types of irregular fighter – guerrilla, partisan ranger, and cavalry raider – became essential parts of the Confederate, and to a lesser extent of the Union war effort. The Confederate irregular forces would develop over time into a serious problem for the Union army, which would respond with a range of antiguerrilla tactics. In this it was never fully successful, and irregular warfare only came to an end after the regular armies of the Confederacy surrendered.

Thousands of armed proslavery Missourians crossed the state line into Kansas to vote for pro-slavery candidates in the 1854 territorial elections. This greatly increased tensions along the border, and soon both sides resorted to guerrilla warfare. The pre-Civil War fighting was mostly by small bands of armed riders raiding the farms of the other side, but it gave the men combat experience that would be useful when the real war started. (Kansas State Historical Society)

The training ground: "Bleeding Kansas"

While formal hostilities opened with the first cannonade against Fort Sumter on April 12, 1861, low-level fighting actually began seven years earlier along the border of Missouri and Kansas. At that time Missouri's population came predominantly from the South; feeling that their agricultural economy, based on slaveholding, had to expand to survive, they looked to the plains of the Kansas Territory as the new frontier. But in 1854 the Kansas-Nebraska Act ruled that the residents of these areas would decide the legal status of slavery. Northern abolitionist leaders encouraged the like-minded to move to the territories, and Emigrant Aid Societies helped hundreds of families to settle there.

While more northerly Nebraska would clearly end up as a "free state," Kansas' status remained a divisive issue, and Missourians started moving into the territory to tip the balance in favor of slavery. A war of words, fought through the press and at street corners and taverns, painted all Missourians as avid slaveholders and all Northern immigrants as rabid abolitionists. Missourians complained that Northern settlers were not bringing their womenfolk or farm tools with them, but only guns. This was an exaggeration, but many settlers did come heavily armed, for fear of the Missourians that Northern newspapers had told them would swamp the territory with slaveholders.

Matters came to a head in the 1854 Kansas territorial elections, when thousands of armed Missourians crossed over the state line to vote for proslavery candidates. Because there were no rules as to what constituted residency, their votes counted; their candidates won by a considerable margin, and did so again in elections the following year. Intimidation soon led to violence. Bands of abolitionist "Jayhawkers" rode into Missouri to raid farms and free slaves, while proslavery "border ruffians" or "Bushwhackers" attacked Kansan farms and wrecked the offices of abolitionist newspapers. The death toll began to mount, and the undermanned Federal garrisons could do little to stop the spreading anarchy. On May 21, 1856, a group

As the fight for the political future of the Kansas Territory heated up, both sides became heavily armed. This 1856 reversed image shows one of the first "Free State batteries" formed by Kansas abolitionists. (Kansas State Historical Society)

of Missourians occupied the abolitionist town of Lawrence, Kansas, seizing weapons, looting homes, and destroying the offices of two newspapers. In reprisal, the abolitionist John Brown and his sons hacked five proslavery men to death in what became known as the Pottawatomie Massacre.

By 1858 power had shifted in favor of the abolitionists because of an increased Federal presence, a continuing influx of Northern immigrants, and large shipments of Sharps rifles from Northern activists. But the raids continued back and forth, growing in strength and skill. Americans on the frontier were getting a field lesson in guerrilla warfare.

Southern and border states and territories, 1860. The numbers indicate the order in which the Confederate states seceded from the Union.

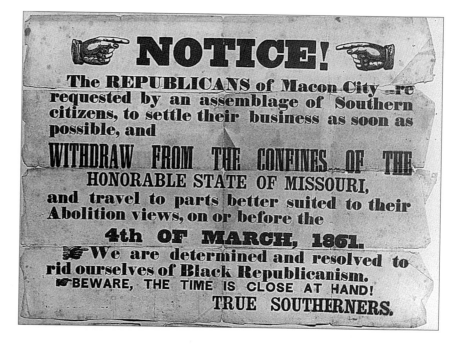

This poster, dating from a month before the attack on Fort Sumter, shows that the Southerners of Macon City, Missouri, did not feel like waiting for the start of the war. (Courtesy State Historical Society of Missouri)

THE IRREGULARS' WAR

EARLY GUERRILLAS:
MARYLAND, VIRGINIA AND TENNESSEE

After the fall of Fort Sumter irregular fighting flared up all across the South and the Border States, and secessionist crowds took over Federal and state armories. In Maryland on April 19, 1861, a pro-Southern mob attacked the 6th Massachusetts Infantry as they changed trains in Baltimore on their way to defend Washington, DC; four soldiers and 12 rioters died, becoming perhaps the first casualties of the war. Bands of secessionists proceeded to burn bridges, cut telegraph lines and tear up track on the Baltimore & Ohio Railroad, isolating the capital until reinforcements arrived later that month. President Lincoln then sent troops to pacify Maryland, and most militant secessionists fled to Virginia to join the Confederate army.

Rioting continued elsewhere, and trains carrying Federal troops in the Border States often found themselves under fire or delayed by sabotage. In the rugged hills of what would later become the state of West Virginia the majority Unionist population found themselves isolated from the Union army, which was preoccupied with protecting the capital and securing Maryland, and Unionist and secessionist guerrilla bands embarked on a bitter low-level conflict that would last throughout the war. This also happened in the Unionist region of eastern Tennessee, where many men fled into Kentucky to join the Union army or stayed home to fight a guerrilla war against secessionists.

The most effective early Unionist partisan in Tennessee was the Rev William Carter, who along with his brother Lt James Carter proposed to burn nine bridges between Bristol, Virginia, and Stevenson, Alabama, blocking supplies to Virginia and opening east Tennessee to Union invasion. On November 8, 1861, Carter's partisans destroyed five of the bridges. The Confederacy moved troops into east Tennessee, declared martial law, and decreed that all bridge-burners would be hanged. A roundup of Unionists netted a thousand prisoners, although

William Carter managed to slip away to Kentucky. Four men who were found guilty were duly hanged next to the newly repaired bridges, and engineers slowed down their trains so that passengers could get a good look at them.

MISSOURI

The state that started the irregular war, Missouri, was an important prize for both sides. Larger than Virginia and more populous than Georgia, Missouri produced more food than all but three of the Confederate states, and St Louis controlled the confluence of the Missouri and Mississippi rivers. Despite their reputation, most Missourians did not want to secede; they wanted a negotiated solution, and consistently voted for moderate candidates. However, Kansas Jayhawkers rarely made any distinction, nor did the Union occupying government; this forced many Missourians into supporting the South when they would have preferred to remain neutral. When the war started the Union command in St Louis quickly ejected the secessionist governor Claiborne Fox Jackson and his supporters from the central part of the state. The Missouri Confederate army, composed of various state guard units and mostly unarmed volunteers led by MajGen Sterling Price, fled to southwest Missouri.

An illustration from *Harper's Weekly* showing the Union sympathizer Col Fry and his collaborators swearing to burn bridges that were vital to Virginia's supply lines; Fry worked with the Carter brothers, whose plan was approved by President Lincoln and funded to the tune of $2,500. In November 1861 the partisans burned five bridges; while Fry personally led more than 30 men against one of them, surprising and capturing the five Confederate sentries and torching the target, other partisans decided that three more bridges were too well guarded – in one case 13 men turned back at the sight of a single sentry. Despite these patchy results the raid struck a serious blow to Southern logistics. (LoC)

Union control of the rivers and railroads made it difficult for Missourians to join Price. In response, Price sent Bushwhackers in civilian clothing to destroy railroad bridges and telegraph lines before he marched back into central Missouri. In his wake rode the Unionist Kansas Senator James Lane and 1,200 Jayhawkers; Lane told his men to strip Missouri of "everything disloyal, from a Shanghai rooster to a Durham cow." On September 23, 1861, they descended on the town of Osceola – one of the largest in the region, with a population of 2,000 – and burned it to the ground for its supposed support of Price. Lack of food and winter clothing, as well as expiring terms of service, forced Price to withdraw and let many of his men go; dispirited by army life, they either went home or became Bushwhackers.

Too weak to move north again, Price sent partisan rangers to recruit for his force, and encouraged Bushwhacker attacks. When the Union command tracked the recruiters' movements and let them gather a sizeable group before attacking them, the mostly unarmed and untrained recruits stood little chance. The Bushwhackers had better luck, destroying infrastructure and ambushing patrols. Unable to guard every mile of track and telegraph line, on December 22 MajGen Henry Halleck, Commander of the Department of Missouri, issued General Order No.31, stating that anyone caught destroying infrastructure would be shot. The ranks of the undeterred Bushwhackers swelled with deserters and paroled prisoners: deserters from Price's army found they could continue the war from the comfort of home, and paroled prisoners disregarded an oath made to a Unionist state government that had been installed by extralegal means.

Union forces were as responsible as General Price for the beginnings of Missouri's guerrilla war. Many hailed from neighboring states, and arrived

convinced that every Missourian was a rebel; they forced local governments to pay for damage done to the railways, and if the money was not forthcoming they took it from shop-owners and citizens. Irate Missourians soon "took to the brush" to fight a guerrilla campaign against the occupying army.

In the meantime, Kansas Jayhawkers continued to raid Missouri, robbing and killing with impunity. Some bands brought armed African Americans with them; as early as November 1861, Jennison's 7th Kansas Cavalry – called "Redlegs" for their distinctive legwear – included a company of blacks led by an escaped Missouri slave. Halleck complained that "The conduct of the forces under Lane and Jennison has done more for the enemy in this State that could have been accomplished by 20,000 of his own army. I receive almost daily complaints of outrages committed by these men in the name of the United States…". (The government ordered Jayhawkers to stay on their side of the state line and relieved Jennison of his command, but the raids continued, and Jennison returned to his unit in 1863.) On March 13, 1862, Halleck issued General Order No.2, declaring that guerrillas were not soldiers but outlaws and would be killed if captured, and consequently this "no quarter" policy was adopted by the Bushwhackers themselves.

On July 22, 1862, the Union command in Missouri issued General Order No.19, requiring every able-bodied man to join the militia "for the purpose of exterminating the guerrillas that infest our state." The order's immediate effect was to make Missouri's entire male population of fighting age choose sides, and a sizeable minority who could not bring themselves to fight for the Union made their way to the Confederate army or joined the guerrillas. One of the latter was a young Frank James, who had served in Price's army until left behind sick during the retreat south. He was captured, paroled, and but for the militia order he might have spent the rest of the war as a peaceful farmer. However, most Missourians did join the militia, and the Union gained 52,000 troops (though some were reluctant soldiers at best, Confederate informers at worst.) Their local knowledge enabled them to target

Frustrated in his attempts to hold Missouri for the Confederacy, MajGen Sterling Price encouraged guerrilla attacks on Union forces there, and sent partisan rangers to recruit men for his army. He was a leading advocate for guerrilla warfare in the Trans-Mississippi theater, and irregular forces fought alongside his army on numerous occasions. (LoC)

Prisons on both sides tended to be crowded and unhealthy, as was this Union prison in Jefferson City, Missouri. Captured rebels were often given the chance to take an oath of loyalty and be released, and many did so to escape the wretched conditions. Few felt obliged to honor their oath, but if they were found taking up arms again they were subject to summary execution. There are numerous reports of guerrillas being found with release papers. (LoC)

true secessionists; but some used the opportunity to settle old scores, and since they were allowed to live off the land when in the field widespread looting further alienated an already hostile populace.

A blockhouse near Aqueduct Bridge, Arlington Heights, Virginia. These simple log forts were quick and easy to construct, yet offered a commanding field of fire over important transport routes. This one even has a crude drawbridge; the walkway connecting the stairs to the doorway could be pulled away, and the lack of windows on the ground floor made it difficult to storm. (LoC)

THE PARTISAN RANGER ACT, APRIL 1862

Confederate President Jefferson Davis disapproved of irregular warfare, judging guerrillas as too hard to control and a drain on the potential ranks of the regular army. In late 1861 Confederate Secretary of War Judah P. Benjamin stated that "Guerrilla companies are not recognized as part of the military organization of the Confederate States," and in early 1862 Gen Joseph E. Johnston drove recruiters for guerrilla bands from his camps. However, faced with the reality of large numbers of Southerners in Union-occupied territory, a lack of sufficient conventional forces, and irregular warfare already raging across the country, the Confederate Congress passed the Partisan Ranger Act on April 21, 1862. This authorized President Davis to commission officers to raise bands of partisan rangers; they would receive the same pay and supplies as regular troops and be subject to the same regulations, but would act independently, and would be paid by the Quartermaster for any captured arms and munitions they delivered. The prospect of independent service seemed exciting and profitable to many young Southern men, and the Partisan Ranger Act would change the way the Civil War was fought.

ARKANSAS

State commanders often modified this act, the most innovative being the new Confederate commander of the Trans-Mississippi Department. In May 1862, MajGen Thomas C. Hindman arrived in Little Rock, Arkansas, at a threatening moment. Price's defeat at Pea Ridge on March 7 had not only crushed the South's hopes of taking Missouri but left Arkansas open to invasion. The Confederacy needed the state's manpower, agricultural produce, and geographical position to threaten the Union west, but most of its trained men had already been transferred east of the Mississippi. There were many Unionists in the Ozark hill country in the north of the state, and the mainly secessionist population of the Arkansas River valley were obviously vulnerable. Hindman imposed martial law, seized as many supplies as he could, and began conscription. Hoping to delay the Union army long enough to rebuild his conventional forces, Hindman started the only guerrilla insurgency instigated and planned by a Confederate state government. His General Order No.17 of June 17, 1862, called upon all men not subject to conscription (as being too old or young, working in essential labor, or living in Union-occupied areas) to form bands of ten or more men to "cut off Federal pickets, scouts, foraging parties, and trains, and kill pilots and others on gunboats and transports...". They would receive pay and supplies, and would be subject to military law and regulation.

Kansas Senator James Lane was quick to realize that there would be a war over slavery, and did his best to hasten its beginning by leading Jayhawking raids into Missouri. It is illegal for a US senator to lead armies in the field, but that did not stop him either before or during the war. Lane was a resident of Lawrence, Kansas, and was himself one of the targets of Quantrill's raid on August 21, 1863. When the Bushwhackers attacked at dawn Lane managed to slip away in his nightshirt, and Quantrill had to content himself with burning down the senator's house. As soon as Lane had secured a horse, gun, and clothes, he organized a pursuit that hounded Quantrill back across the state line. (Kansas State Historical Society)

By August 1862, Hindman had raised 18,000 regular and 5,000 irregular troops. When a flotilla of Union gunboats tried to open up the White River in northeast Arkansas to Union shipping they were driven off by constant fire from guerrilla sharpshooters, and the guerrillas swarming through the northern half of the state helped keep the Union forces from taking the Arkansas River valley and Little Rock for another year. However, Arkansas would come to regret Hindman's orders: the government was never able to control the guerrillas, who would become more like outlaws than Confederate irregulars.

THE SPIRAL OF REPRISALS

By the end of 1862, Missouri and northern Arkansas had settled into a pattern of guerrilla attacks and Union reprisals that differed only in their ever-increasing viciousness. The Union command imprisoned the womenfolk of known Bushwhackers and pressured their families to move south into Confederate territory, in the hopes that the guerrillas would follow. When a Kansas City prison collapsed on August 14, 1863, and killed five such women, the Bushwhackers flew into a rage, convinced that the Federals had murdered them – an unthinkable crime in those days. Several members of William Quantrill's band lost relatives in the prison collapse, and on August 21 they descended on Lawrence, Kansas, a hotspot of abolitionism and home to Senator Lane. Shouting "Remember Osceola!" and the names of their dead relatives, they indulged in a drunken orgy of looting and killing that left nearly 200 men and boys dead in the streets and much of the town in flames. In response to this worst atrocity against civilians in the Civil War, four days later BrigGen Thomas Ewing issued General Order No.11; this removed virtually the entire population from three western Missouri counties and a portion of another. Union troops in charge of this mass eviction, including Jennison's Redlegs, took the opportunity to pillage and burn, and for decades afterwards this region was known as the "Burnt District."

CAVALRY RAIDERS: MORGAN AND FORREST, 1862

In Kentucky and Tennessee, perhaps the Confederacy's two greatest cavalry raiders – BrigGens John Hunt Morgan and Nathan Bedford Forrest – began major operations.

At the start of the war Morgan commanded a militia in Lexington, Kentucky, and when that state declared neutrality he moved them south to join the Confederate army. He became a captain in October 1861, and immediately began targeting outposts and bridges behind Federal lines in Kentucky and Tennessee, sometimes dressing his men in Union uniforms. Nathan Bedford Forrest had enlisted in the Confederate army in Tennessee as a private, but soon proved his great ability as a scout, and was given authority to raise a cavalry battalion; collecting men from several states, he too was active by the end of 1861.

In summer 1862 MajGen Braxton Bragg ordered both these officers on a two-pronged raid in advance of his anticipated invasion of eastern Tennessee and Kentucky. Their aim was to disrupt communications, delay Federal troop movements, and destroy the opposing cavalry. Morgan's 2nd Kentucky Cavalry, along with units from Georgia and Texas, set out on July 4, winning a series of small engagements and destroying almost a million dollars' worth of property. In Tennessee on July 11, Forrest's amalgamated force targeted the railroad center of Murfreesboro, where he destroyed half a million dollars' worth of property

THE VOLUNTARY MANNER IN WHICH SOME OF THE SOUTHERN VOLUNTEERS ENLIST.

A Northern cartoon lampooning Southern recruitment methods; one man lies on the floor drunk, while another is forced to volunteer at bayonet-point. In actuality, strong-arm tactics by recruiters on both sides caused significant numbers of men to hide out in the wilderness. Some resorted to banditry, while others fought the war in their own way as guerrillas. (LoC)

After Quantrill's raid Lawrence, Kansas, was left little more than a smoking ruin. (LoC)

including supplies and rolling stock. Later that summer the two commanders harassed the Union Army of Ohio's move towards Chattanooga. Working in groups ranging from ten to 600 men, they wore down BrigGen Don Carlos Buell's advance by targeting his long and poorly guarded supply lines, forcing him to withdraw.

In response to the raids local Union commanders raised Home Guard units. These tended to be poorly trained and led, but did free up regular troops for combat duty. Buell also started raising more cavalry, and built a system of blockhouses to protect key locations, especially on the railroads. The little forts proved effective against guerrillas, but barely slowed cavalry raiders equipped with artillery. Bragg reorganized his own cavalry, dividing them into "regular" brigades attached to infantry corps, and two "partisan" brigades under Morgan and Forrest to concentrate on raiding. While raids were a part of both Confederate and later Union strategy in all three theaters, only the Confederate army in the Western theater had units specifically dedicated to such missions.

By December 1862, Bragg had concentrated 40,000 Confederates at Murfreesboro in anticipation of an advance by MajGen William Rosecrans' slightly larger force. Once again Bragg sent his two raiders off to harry the

A THE BURNING OF LAWRENCE, KANSAS; AUGUST 21, 1863

On the night of 20/21 August 1863, William Quantrill led about 450 guerrillas across the border from western Missouri to Lawrence, Kansas, a center for abolitionism and home to Jayhawker leader Jim Lane. They used captive local farmers as guides; when each guide got past their area of familiarity they shot him and kidnapped another. After working their way through ten guides, the guerrillas galloped into Lawrence in the morning, finding the local Union garrison absent. They proceeded to sack and burn the town, and killed about 200 men and boys (though they did not molest women). When Union cavalry rode to Lawrence the Bushwhackers fought a running battle back across the state line, losing about 40 men before splitting up and disappearing into Missouri's thick woodlands.

1: Quantrill wears a slouch hat and the typical "guerrilla shirt" favored by Trans-Mississippi Bushwhackers. He carries a Sharps rifle, a pair of Colt Navy revolvers, and a Bowie knife, all favorite weapons of the guerrilla.

2: "Bloody Bill" Anderson, then one of Quantrill's captains, wears his hair long in typical Bushwhacker fashion, and is also armed with .36cal Colt Navy revolvers, which the guerrillas found handier for use on horseback then the heavier .44cal Army.

3: Quantrill's men fired the town, typically using sticks with cotton wads soaked in turpentine. They favored red guerrilla shirts, and in addition to several revolvers some carried shotguns, sawed to a shorter length for ease of use on horseback.

A warning to the "common foe of mankind – the guerrilla and bush-whacker", stating that every time a telegraph line was cut the Union command would hang a Bushwhacker prisoner and burn the house of a nearby secessionist. Such harsh tactics did little to discourage Bushwhackers, and much to stoke hatred among civilians. (Courtesy of the Littlejohn Collection, Wofford College)

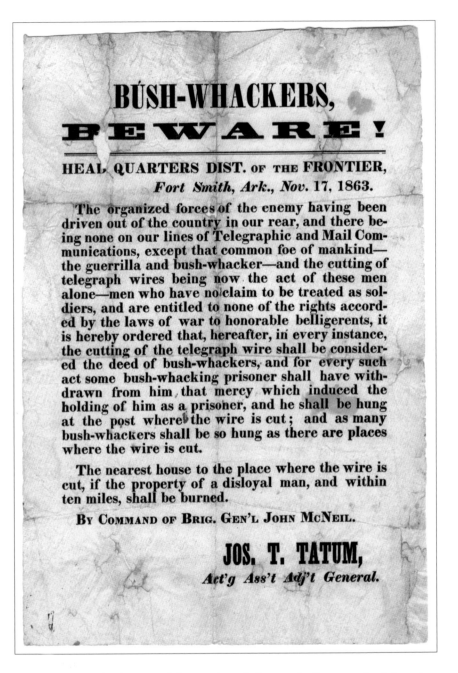

BUSH-WHACKERS, BEWARE!

HEAD QUARTERS DIST. of the FRONTIER,
Fort Smith, Ark., Nov. 17, 1863.

The organized forces of the enemy having been driven out of the country in our rear, and there being none on our lines of Telegraphic and Mail Communications, except that common foe of mankind—the guerrilla and bush-whacker—and the cutting of telegraph wires being now the act of these men alone—men who have no claim to be treated as soldiers, and are entitled to none of the rights accorded by the laws of war to honorable belligerents, it is hereby ordered that, hereafter, in every instance, the cutting of the telegraph wire shall be considered the deed of bush-whackers, and for every such act some bush-whacking prisoner shall have withdrawn from him, that mercy which induced the holding of him as a prisoner, and he shall be hung at the post where the wire is cut; and as many bush-whackers shall be so hung as there are places where the wire is cut.

The nearest house to the place where the wire is cut, if the property of a disloyal man, and within ten miles, shall be burned.

By Command of Brig. Gen'l John McNeil.

JOS. T. TATUM,
Act'g Ass't Adj't General.

Union rear in the hopes of destroying their supply lines, and of drawing enough cavalry away to blind the Union army. As before, Bragg staggered the raids, with Forrest setting out on December 11 and Morgan on December 22. Forrest led 2,100 horsemen and four cannon into western Tennessee to ravage the Mobile & Ohio Railroad, forcing Rosecrans to send cavalry in pursuit. The Confederate raiders defeated several Union detachments, whose fleeing soldiers spread exaggerated reports of enemy numbers and caused the 20,000 Union troops in that region to dig in. With his enemy thus immobilized, Forrest was free to burn supplies and tear up rails.

Morgan's mission was to ride into central Kentucky and burn a pair of large railroad trestles at Muldraugh's Hill. His 3,100 men and seven cannon won a few quick skirmishes and reached the trestles on December 28, where they found that the 700-strong Union garrison had not completed their fortifications and lacked artillery. A three-hour bombardment convinced them to surrender, and Morgan destroyed both trestles and a large quantity of military stores. Union forces converged on the 2nd Kentucky from three directions, but superior horses and a fortuitous snowstorm allowed the Rebels to make their escape. The trestles would take five weeks to rebuild.

While the Union had begun implementing an antiraiding strategy before these so-called "Christmas Raids," it was not fully in place. As at Muldraugh's Hill, many blockhouses were incomplete or not equipped with cannon; Union cavalry had not yet been fully reinforced, and those that were present were spread thin guarding vital sites and hunting guerrillas. However, despite the huge boost to Southern morale, Rosecrans had expected raids on his supply lines and had stockpiled months of stores at his advanced positions, so the destruction of the Muldraugh's Hill trestles was

only a minor inconvenience. Moreover, Bragg's two "partisan" brigades accounted for half his cavalrymen, and their absence behind Federal lines blinded his own movements in the exact same way that he intended to blind Rosecrans. This lack of proper cavalry support was a contributing factor to his inability to defeat Rosecrans at the bloody battle of Stones River (December 31 to January 3, 1862/63).

While the Northern press denounced Confederate raiders as bandits and arsonists, it lauded Union cavalry raiders such as Col Benjamin Grierson as heroes. The Southern press, of course, did the reverse, and contributed to the image of the chivalric Southern cavalryman that lasts to this day. (LoC)

Meanwhile, control of western Virginia seesawed between the two sides. When Lee's invasion of Maryland in late summer 1862 drove the Federals out of northern Virginia, Confederate cavalry raiders, partisans under Col John Imboden, and local guerrillas all swept through the area. The Federals soon retook the region, and at the end of the year Imboden's men and other bands were reincorporated into the regular army; Capt John McNeill's group in western Virginia was one of the few allowed to continue independent operations, although they too lost their charter later. One of their primary targets was the Baltimore & Ohio Railroad, an essential lifeline to the Federal capital stretching vulnerably through the forested mountains of western Virginia.

CONSEQUENCES OF THE CONSCRIPTION ACT

A significant milestone for Unionist guerrillas came with the Confederate Conscription Act of April 16, 1862, which made military service compulsory for men aged 18 to 35. This had the same effect as the militia act in Missouri – it forced civilians to choose sides, and as a consequence Union guerrillas sprang up in western North and South Carolina, northern Georgia, Alabama's northern hill country, parts of Mississippi, and the swamps of Louisiana and Florida. Secret societies such as the Heroes of America and the Peace Society operated across the South. Texas Unionists had been passive until the conscription law,

Guerrillas discovered that trains made easy targets; robbing them denied supplies to the enemy and could earn the guerrillas a handsome profit. Union commanders soon recognized the need to provide armor plating for locomotives, and to attach armored artillery cars front and rear; sometimes these were supplemented with rifle-cars – boxcars roughly protected by inner walls of railroad ties, loopholed for infantry escorts. Cars such as this were proof against small-arms fire but not against artillery, and the locomotive boiler and cab were always vulnerable. (*Frank Leslie's Illustrated Newspaper*)

but now hundreds fled to the North or formed guerrilla bands. In the summer of 1862 they made a "Peace Plot" to separate north Texas from the rest of the state, but the Confederate government suppressed it, hanging 65 "renegados" in Gainesville on a single day. Another Unionist rebellion in the spring of 1863 was suppressed by a partisan band of Texan Indian-fighters who, according to a local newspaper, "never took prisoners but did take scalps."

An unpopular clause in the Conscription Act exempted men owning 20 or more slaves, leading to the widespread impression that it was a "rich man's war and a poor man's fight." In the western Carolinas draft-dodgers or deserters roamed in bands of 50 to 500, building forts, occupying towns, and being helped

B ANDERSON'S BAIT-AND-AMBUSH TACTICS AFTER CENTRALIA; SEPTEMBER 27, 1864

On that date, "Bloody Bill" Anderson raided the little town of Centralia, Missouri, with 30 men before rendezvousing with the remainder of his approximately 250-strong force and moving southeast. At 4pm, Union Major A.V.E. Johnston led 158 mounted riflemen of the 39th Missouri Infantry into Centralia; he had been hunting the guerrillas since the previous day, and now he unwisely divided his force, leaving one group to restore order in the village while he led 120 men in pursuit.

1: A mile outside of Centralia he spotted ten riders galloping away, but this was a ruse – Dave Poole's men were the bait to draw Johnston into an ambush.

2: The Union soldiers followed Poole's riders over a low rise , and saw a line of about 90 of Anderson's guerrillas at the bottom of the slope; each Rebel stood by his horse, one foot in the stirrup.

3: Johnston's men carried single-shot Enfield rifle-muskets that were difficult to reload on horseback, so he ordered them to dismount and form a line. A quarter of his men acted as horse-holders, each leading his own and three other horses to the rear ('xxx'). Poole's riders had reached the bottom of

the meadow and took position behind Anderson's line; meanwhile, other parties led by Thrailkill, T. and G. Todd and Gordon – perhaps 70 men on each flank – remained concealed in the edge of the woods.

4: On Anderson's order, the Bushwhackers swung into the saddle, drew their revolvers, and charged. Johnston's men got off one volley but it went high – a common mistake for inexperienced men firing downhill – and killed only three guerrillas. Within moments, Anderson's men had ridden over the Union line, slaughtering them with repeated shots from their six-shooter revolvers as the soldiers tried to reload or fix bayonets. Major Johnston traded shots with Jesse James before James killed him. The other guerrillas now came out of the woods and followed Anderson's charge.

5: Union horse-holders galloped away, but the Bushwhackers, riding much better horses than the mounted infantrymen's nags, caught them easily and gunned them down.

The guerrillas then galloped back to Centralia and finished off the rest of Johnston's command. The 39th Missouri lost two officers and 114 enlisted men killed, two wounded, and six missing; the low number of wounded was due to Anderson's "no quarter" policy – some of the dead were scalped and a few beheaded.

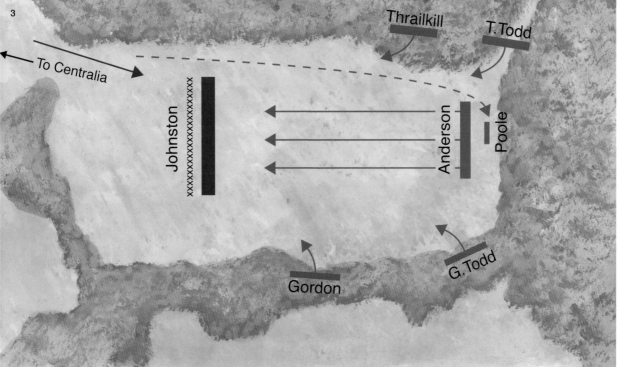

Thrailkill

T.Todd

To Centralia

Johnston

Anderson

Poole

Gordon

G.Todd

A Union foraging party returns to camp. While the artist has depicted a rich plunder of produce and animals, in reality forage became increasingly scarce as the war dragged on and the civilian population in contested areas were looted into destitution by both sides. (*Frank Leslie's Illustrated Newspaper*)

by a mostly sympathetic populace. In such gangs they ambushed patrols, robbed plantations and mails, and prevented the collection of taxes. Along the coasts they aided Union blockaders and raiders, and rustled cattle to feed Union troops and Unionist refugees, causing a shortage for the Confederate army. By 1864 the Confederate governor of Florida was afraid to leave the capital at Tallahassee for fear of capture. The Florida militia was unequal to the problem, so in April 1864 a Confederate regiment set out to destroy these bands; they only managed to burn the homes of various Tories, causing an angry group of "500 Union men, deserters, and negroes" to attack the area around Gainesville.

In Louisiana, guerrilla warfare began after the fall of New Orleans on May 1, 1862. On May 28 a boat from Adm David Farragut's flagship USS *Hartford* came ashore at Baton Rouge to do some laundry; 40 guerrillas hiding on the landing opened up with buckshot, wounding one officer and two sailors. An irate Farragut shelled the town, killing one woman and wounding two more and destroying several public buildings. This incident was repeated at Donaldsville several months later. The Confederate governor of Louisiana called a halt to the firing on boats, and public complaints about irregular forces being as bad as the Federals caused the government to disband the partisans and put them into regular service. The guerrillas, however, continued to thrive. When they tried to stop freed blacks from harvesting cotton to sell to New England and Britain, the blacks fought back by raiding white settlements; in May 1863 Confederates hanged 50 of them for raiding in St Mary's Parish.

1863: UNION PRECAUTIONS, CONFEDERATE RAIDS

The year 1863 saw a rise in guerrilla activity in the Trans-Mississippi. In response, the Union command in Missouri and northern Arkansas created a system of defense in depth. Each county got its own garrison, generally centered on the county seat, where the large brick courthouse could be fortified. Detachments of cavalry were assigned to all major towns and scoured their local areas; any sighting of Bushwhackers would be communicated to all other posts, and the cavalry would try to converge on them. Large numbers of blockhouses were built to protect vulnerable targets; considering the Bushwhackers' lack of artillery and the numerous examples of their inability to take fortified positions, it is perhaps surprising that such comprehensive precautions were not taken earlier.

The system did have its weaknesses, however. Post commanders had to be careful how many men they sent out on patrol: if the party was too small, it might be overcome, but if too big, the post itself might be dangerously undermanned. Keeping the scattered posts supplied also became a dangerous and expensive commitment. Nevertheless, reports from the last two years of the war show an increasing number of engagements in which Union troops either won or at least forced the Bushwhackers to retreat. While some bands made foolish and costly attacks on Union courthouses and blockhouses, most concentrated on hitting supply trains, robbing and killing Unionist civilians, attacking small and undefended towns, destroying railroads and telegraph lines, and shooting at steamboats. The attacks on riverboats became so bad that shipping costs rose to nearly unaffordable levels, and all steamboats had to be armored; at some times and places rail and river traffic stopped altogether.

As in the Western theater, the Trans-Mississippi Confederates conducted several raids in 1863. Brigadier-General John Sappington Marmaduke twice launched raids from Arkansas into Missouri in futile attempts to keep the Federal army from advancing and taking Little Rock. While his two raids did

Runaway slaves drained the South's always critical labor pool and provided the Federals with valuable workmen. They eagerly attached themselves to the Union troops they encountered, but if guerrillas caught them straying from the main column they generally shot them on the spot. The Federal government was at first hesitant to use African Americans as soldiers, and it was against President Lincoln's express orders that Jayhawker leader Jim Lane raised the 1st Kansas Colored Volunteers among free blacks from Kansas as well as runaways from Missouri and Arkansas, some of whom had been liberated during his many raids. The 1st Kansas Colored defeated a group of Missouri Bushwhackers at Island Mound on October 29, 1862, becoming the first black regiment of the US Army to see combat. (*Frank Leslie's Illustrated Newspaper*)

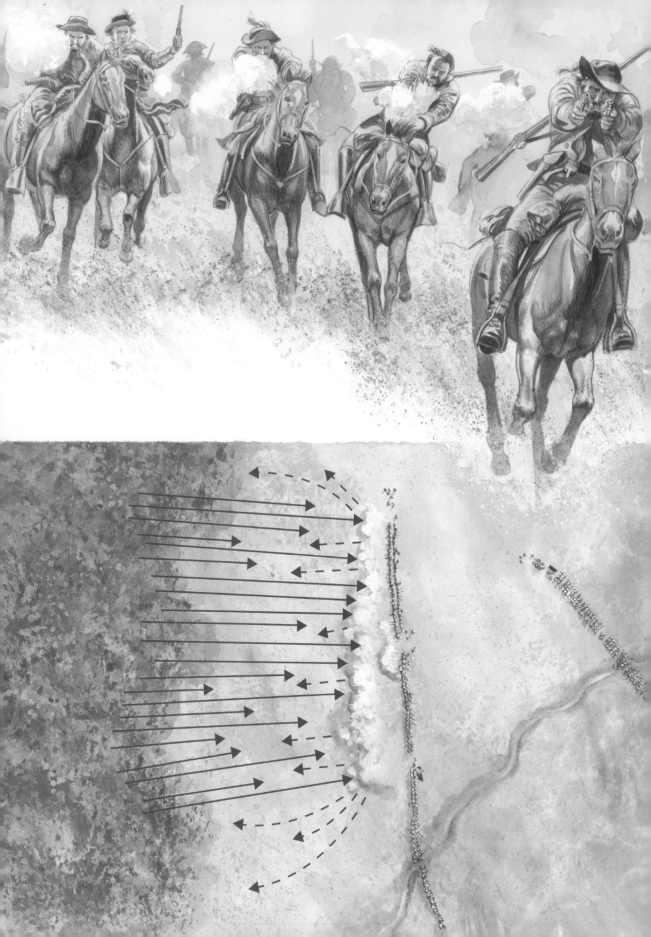

much damage to infrastructure, Marmaduke had a tendency to get bogged down in pitched battles and assaults on forts. More successful was BrigGen Joseph Orville Shelby's Missouri raid, which rode without supply wagons, avoided major engagements, and sent scouts ahead to gather intelligence about road conditions and Union troop positions. Shelby destroyed nearly two million dollars' worth of infrastructure and supplies and captured 1,200 small arms, at a time when many Arkansas Confederates were unarmed or went into the firing line with squirrel-guns.

A harsh winter stopped any major raiding in the Western theater until spring 1863, and gave the Union army time to complete its antiraiding precautions. The addition of several more regiments gave the Union greater ability to protect its rear areas, and fortifications were completed and provided with artillery. Rosecrans also created a large cavalry corps, well armed and separate from the infantry, to chase down raiders. Regular patrols by gunboats along the region's many rivers provided additional firepower.

The Union cavalry had now grown strong enough to conduct deep raids of their own, both to destroy Southern infrastructure and to distract Confederate cavalry. In April 1863 Col Abel Streight led 1,700 men into Alabama; these raiders were poorly supplied, riding mules rather than horses, but they got deep into the state, destroying infrastructure and trying to arouse the Unionist population in the northern hills. Forrest hunted Streight's command down, trapped them and forced them to surrender, but the exhausting chase wore down his mounts and kept him from raiding for the rest of that spring. His victory also earned him a promotion that attached him to the regular army. The South had temporarily lost the special services of one of its most daring raiders, and would soon lose another.

Despite not having Forrest to conduct raids in his support, BrigGen Morgan decided to strike into the heart of the North, cutting through Kentucky, Indiana and Ohio. He feared the Confederate high command would forbid such a risky venture, so he obtained permission only for a raid against Louisville, Kentucky, revealing his true plans to only a few close associates. On July 1, 1863 he set out with 2,460 men, mostly mounted on Kentucky thoroughbreds, and four cannon. As soon as he entered Ohio he found the Union defense vastly improved. Rather than fleeing at the sight of him, Home Guard units put up a dogged resistance from fortified bridges and stone buildings. Union cavalry pursued him tirelessly, showing a new tenacity and skill, while gunboats prowled every river. Morgan's troopers fought well and rode hard, and his telegraph operator George Ellsworth worked overtime sending misleading signals to the Union forces, but the entire countryside was on the alert; riders carried news to every town and hamlet, while Home Guard units blared on conch shells to warn

C MOSBY'S "CHARGE AND SKEDADDLE"

A typical tactic of Mosby's partisan rangers was "the skedaddle," used against a numerically superior force to disorient them and delay pursuit. Mosby's cavalrymen would charge the enemy line in a loose group as fast as their individual horses could carry them, creating a large mass of riders kicking up dust and clouding the air with gunsmoke from their rapidly-fired revolvers. This gave the impression that they had more men than they did, assuring a psychological advantage over the enemy, and the fusillade of pistol shots at close range inflicted heavy casualties. When the Union troops reorganized or realized that they outnumbered their attackers, the Rebel cavalry would "skedaddle," galloping away individually in all directions. Each man would proceed to a predetermined rendezvous, where they would regroup to either attack again or withdraw. Interestingly, one of Mosby's men wrote that the skedaddle was never actually given as a command; the riders were well-trained enough that everyone knew instinctively when to break off.

their men. Morgan managed to avoid many Union detachments and defeated others, but what started as a raid quickly became a chase.

When he tried to cross the Ohio River to the safety of western Virginia on July 19 he was surrounded by Federal forces, and lost nearly 600 men killed or captured before the rest could fight their way out. Morgan led his men northwards in search of another crossing-place, but parts of his exhausted command were defeated and captured one by one until, on July 29, Morgan himself surrendered the remnants of his force. Although it destroyed huge amounts of property Morgan's "Great Raid" had achieved little real damage to the Federal war effort. Major-General Ambrose Burnside had to divert some men to help with the chase, thus delaying the start of his campaign in eastern Tennessee, but the annihilation of Morgan's command meant that Burnside had no need to commit many troops to protect his rear once he did set out. For the Confederates, the raid made great newspaper copy but cost them one of their best raiders and nearly 2,500 of their best cavalry. Morgan and some of his officers managed to escape from prison and make their way back to the South, but he was never again trusted with an important command.

1863–64: MOSBY, THE LAST GREAT RAIDER

As Morgan's star fell, that of John Singleton Mosby was ascending. A lawyer from solid Virginia stock, he had enlisted as a private, but his talent soon earned him a position as MajGen J.E.B. Stuart's most trusted scout, providing excellent intelligence during a number of campaigns. In March 1863 he was commissioned a captain of partisan rangers and given the task of fighting

Members of the Delaware tribe acting as Federal scouts. Native Americans fought for both sides, and provided some of the best scouts and irregular forces for the Confederacy. Confederate Indians made numerous raids into Union-held Missouri and northern Arkansas, and were among the last to lay down their arms at war's end. (*Frank Leslie's Illustrated Newspaper*)

behind Federal lines in Virginia. His main role was intelligence-gathering and attacking Union lines of communication in support of the Army of Northern Virginia. His 43rd Virginia Cavalry Battalion soon made a name for itself by capturing BrigGen Edwin H. Stoughton at Fairfax Court House. Accurate intelligence of Union troop dispositions, a small group of disciplined and fearless riders, and a clear objective made this raid a success, and a model for others to come. That May, Mosby attacked the supply lines of the Army of the Potomac and provided intelligence for Lee's Gettysburg campaign; acting as a screening force, his rangers so confused and blinded MajGen Hooker that Lee was able to get a few days' head start into Pennsylvania.

After Lee's defeat at Gettysburg (July 1–3), partisans in western Virginia refocused their efforts towards interrupting traffic on the Baltimore & Ohio and Orange & Alexandria railroads – the first to delay the transfer of Union troops to Tennessee, the second to stop Union movement against the battered Army of Northern Virginia. However, the Union command had placed an entire infantry corps along the lines, manned every train, and developed faster techniques for repairing damaged rails, so rail traffic was never stopped for more than a day at a time.

Pressed for men, Gen Lee and other commanders convinced the Confederate government to revoke the Partisan Ranger Act in February 1864, and to muster all irregular units into the army. This did not affect the guerrillas, over whom the government had no control, but it did lead to a sharp decline in partisan ranger warfare.

The government made an exception in the case of Mosby's 43rd Virginia Cavalry, whose capability, self-control, and strategic importance ensured them special treatment. As Confederate forces withdrew from northern Virginia, Mosby's base of operations between the Blue Ridge and Bull Run mountains – less than 50 miles from the Federal capital – became virtually a separate command, dubbed "Mosby's Confederacy." Mosby continued to harass the Federals even as they pushed towards Richmond, raiding from western Virginia to the very gates of Washington DC in an attempt to relieve pressure on Lee. Mosby also attacked blockhouses and turned on small detachments sent to catch him, and repeatedly hit the Baltimore & Ohio Railroad.

In Kentucky, guerrillas increased in number. The governor tried to stop them by levying fines on secessionists, with predictable results. By the summer of 1864 the situation had become so bad that Lincoln put the entire state under martial law, and departmental commander MajGen Stephen Burbridge began executing four Confederate prisoners for every Union soldier or civilian killed by the irregulars.

In Tennessee, Morgan made new raids, but was himself killed on September 4, 1864. Rebel guerrilla Champ Ferguson ranged across the Cumberland Mountains, where Unionists and secessionists fought a bitter, family-feud style campaign. Ferguson's character is a matter of controversy; many Southerners think he was an effective local leader, while most historians paint him as a sadistic killer who murdered more than 100 men. The law favored the second perspective (see below).

THE FINAL MONTHS

By 1865, many cavalry raiders were dead or leading tattered remnants of their earlier forces. Some of the best partisan ranger leaders had also been killed, and the guerrillas had descended into a state of semi-savagery. In Virginia,

LtGen Jubal Early ordered Harry Gilmor to bring together all the guerrilla bands for an attack on the Baltimore & Ohio Railroad to stop Sheridan from transferring troops to Grant, but the other bands would not recognize Gilmor's authority; spies tracked him down, and he was captured on February 5.

On February 21, McNeill's rangers approached Cumberland, Maryland on the morning after a snowstorm; they overpowered three Union pickets and obtained the countersign, then moved into town and captured MajGens George Crook and Benjamin Kelley. On March 2, Sheridan mopped up the remains of Early's army and moved to join Grant. Mosby was now truly alone in northern and western Virginia. He captured nearly all of the Loudon Rangers, a company of Virginia Unionists who had dogged him for two years, but on April 21 he resigned himself to the inevitable and disbanded his unit. As news of Lee's surrender spread others started doing the same; one by one the bands of guerrillas and partisans who had harried Union forces throughout the war broke up and went home.

THE LEADERS

GUERRILLA LEADERS

William "Bloody Bill" Anderson (Confederate) A Missourian and one of Quantrill's (q.v.) captains, Anderson seems to have gone insane after one of his sisters died in a Kansas City prison collapse. He often charged into battle muttering her name and frothing at the mouth, yet he remained a cunning tactician. His penchant for killing civilians and scalping soldiers earned him the reputation as the most merciless of the Bushwhackers. After Quantrill's group broke up in the winter of 1863/64 Anderson led his own band – including the James brothers – and was killed on October 26, 1864.

Champ Ferguson (Confederate) A Kentucky farmer accused of murdering a sheriff before the war, Ferguson organized a guerrilla unit in the mountains of eastern Tennessee to attack Unionist civilians and fight "Tinker Dave" Beaty (q.v.). He occasionally worked with Confederate forces and may have been made an official partisan ranger, although this is debated. He developed a reputation for sadism, and at the end of the war was found guilty of 53 murders and executed. Ferguson himself claimed that the number was more like 100, although he protested he was only doing his duty.

William Quantrill (Confederate) An Ohio schoolteacher who lived in Kansas during the border wars, Quantrill became a notorious guerrilla. He started out with ten men protecting Jackson County, western Missouri, from Jayhawker raids, and quickly gathered more recruits. During the Civil War his group sometimes numbered in the hundreds. They killed soldiers and civilians alike, and on August 21, 1863 they destroyed Lawrence, Kansas, killing about 200 mostly unarmed men and boys. His band broke up due to infighting in the winter of 1863/64, and he was killed in Kentucky on June 6, 1865.

PARTISAN RANGER LEADERS

"Tinker Dave" Beaty (Union) An illiterate tinker from eastern Tennessee, in 1862 he formed Beaty's Independent Scouts, a partisan group recognized and supplied by the Federal army. Ranging from a couple of dozen men to about 100, it attracted deserters from both sides. Beaty helped secure the roads from Confederate guerrillas, but spent much of his time harassing "enemy civilians"; he also murdered soldiers on both sides for their weapons, and ambushed supply wagons for loot. A bitter enemy of Champ Ferguson (q.v.), Beaty finally had the satisfaction of being a witness for the prosecution at Ferguson's postwar murder trial.

Nathan Bedford Forrest (Confederate) A wealthy plantation-owner and slave-dealer from Tennessee, Forrest enlisted as a private and rose to the rank of lieutenant-general. Nicknamed "The Wizard of the Saddle" for his daring raids and ability to trick, outmaneuver, and outfight his Union opponents, he earned a reputation as one of the best generals in American history and one of the first proponents of mobile warfare. He led his troops both as an independent command and as a part of larger armies. His deep raids into Union territory destroyed large amounts of supplies and tied up thousands of Federal troops. After the war he had an unclear association with the Ku Klux Klan, being named honorary Grand Wizard in 1867 before distancing himself from that organization.

Harry Gilmor (Confederate) A Baltimore City police commissioner before the war, Gilmor became a Confederate major and led "Gilmor's Raiders," a partisan group in Maryland and West Virginia. His most famous raid on July 9–11, 1864 destroyed two trains and damaged a trestle at Magnolia Station, MD, and captured Union MajGen William Franklin. Gilmor himself was captured on February 4, 1865.

Dr Charles Jennison (Union) Born in New York and raised in Wisconsin, Jennison moved to Kansas during the 1850s border war. In 1861 he was commissioned lieutenant-colonel of the 7th Kansas Volunteer Cavalry, known as "Jennison's Redlegs." He plundered the farms of Missouri secessionists and brought their slaves to freedom in Kansas. Jennison had a penchant for stealing horses; when horses went up for sale west of the Mississippi, their pedigree was often referred to as "out of Missouri by Jennison."

James Lane (Union) Also known as the "Grim Chieftain," this Indiana politician moved to "Bleeding Kansas" and became a leader of the radical abolitionists, rising to become a senator. He was the most organized of the early Jayhawkers, leading numerous raids both before and during the war at the head of 3rd and 4th Kansas Volunteer Infantry and 5th Kansas Cavalry.

Col John Singleton Mosby led one of the only partisan ranger units not to be disbanded by the repeal of the Partisan Ranger Act in February 1864. His record of success and firm discipline over his troops meant that he was more valuable in independent command than within the depleted Confederate army. The repeal did little to ease the Confederacy's shortage of troops; the partisan rangers were relatively few in number and some failed to rally, while guerrillas naturally ignored the order. (LoC)

John McNeill (Confederate) A prosperous farmer, McNeill became a successful Confederate partisan in West Virginia, though rarely leading more than 100 men. Their main aims were to harass local Union troops, attack the Baltimore & Ohio Railroad, and bring livestock from the rich Shenandoah Valley to the Confederate Army; they also acted as guides for regular Confederate forces. McNeill died from wounds suffered during a raid on November 10, 1864. His son Jesse took over leadership of the band, and gained notoriety for capturing two Union generals.

John Hunt Morgan (Confederate) Born in Alabama but raised in Kentucky, Morgan served as a cavalry private in the Mexican War before becoming a successful businessman. During the Civil War he rose to the rank of brigadier-general. His July 1863 raid through Kentucky, Indiana, and Ohio penetrated further north than any other Confederate force, but he and most of his men were captured. He escaped from prison with six of his officers and got back to the South, where he formed another cavalry unit and led more raids until he was killed on September 4, 1864.

Brigadier General John Hunt Morgan was one of the South's greatest cavalry raiders in 1862, but suffered from an overconfidence that led him to raid deep into Indiana and Ohio the following July, resulting in the loss of his entire command. (LoC)

John Singleton Mosby (Confederate) A Virginia lawyer known as the "Grey Ghost of the Confederacy," Mosby quickly rose from private to lieutenant-colonel. In 1863 he was authorized to raise the 43rd Battalion Virginia Cavalry, a partisan ranger unit. He became increasingly independent as his area of operations in northwestern Virginia became isolated from Lee's army. His command kept a portion of Virginia out of Federal hands until the end of the war.

Joseph Porter (Confederate) Born in Kentucky and raised in Missouri, Porter was assigned in 1862 to gather recruits in northeast Missouri, an area cut off from the Confederate command in Arkansas. While initially successful, his force fought several running battles with Union forces and was scattered. He was killed on February 18, 1863.

Joseph Orville Shelby (Confederate) The most accomplished cavalry raider in the Trans-Mississippi theater, Shelby grew up in Kentucky before moving to Missouri and becoming a successful farmer and businessman. He was one of many Missourians who voted in the controversial Kansas elections, and when the war started he recruited a cavalry troop at his own expense. He later recruited and led the 5th Missouri Cavalry ("Iron Brigade") and conducted several independent raids. He rose to the rank of brigadier-general, and fled to Mexico rather than surrender to Federal forces.

Meriwether Jeff Thompson (Confederate) Nicknamed the "Swamp Fox," Thompson fought Union troops from his hideouts in the swamps along the Mississippi River in southeastern Missouri and northeastern Arkansas. Born in Virginia and later a resident of Missouri, he became brigadier-general of the military district of Southeast Missouri. His men conducted hit-and-run raids on Federal outposts and boats, and occasionally gathered in numbers of more than 1,000 to fight small battles.

ORGANIZATION & TACTICS

LEADERSHIP

Guerrilla bands ranged in strength from a handful to hundreds of men, but each was a loose conglomeration unified by a charismatic leader. A guerrilla leader had to be brave, tough, successful, but most of all a hero to the mostly young farm boys who followed him. Leading, not to mention controlling, a rough group of guerrillas took a man who led from the front and fought at least as well as the average member of his group. Since he did not enjoy membership of the officer class of the organized army, his authority was not automatic but entirely personal.

Thomas C. Reynolds, Confederate Governor-in-exile of Missouri, advised Quantrill in February 1864 that both sides had lost their patience with guerrilla warfare and that if he wanted to further his career he should enter the regular Confederate service. He warned him that "All authority over undisciplined bands is short-lived. The history of every guerrilla chief has been the same. He either becomes the slave of his men, or if he attempts to control them, some officer or some private rises up, disputes his authority, gains the men, and puts him down." That May, Reynolds' prediction came true. George Todd, one of Quantrill's officers who felt he deserved more authority than he had been given, drew a gun on Quantrill in front of his men and asked if he feared him. Facing humiliation or death, Quantrill chose humiliation and replied that he did. That night he slunk away from camp, leading only a small fraction of his band; he would never have a sizable following again.

In fact, Quantrill's authority had been eroding ever since the Lawrence massacre. Some guerrillas were shocked at the brutality of the attack, while others wanted to carry out more such expeditions and rankled under what little discipline Quantrill imposed. The showdown with Todd only made plain Quantrill's lack of true authority. Another of his captains, "Bloody Bill" Anderson, also left Quantrill and took the most savage elements of the group with him. They would descend further into barbarity by taking scalps, routinely killing helpless civilians, and even assaulting women – something considered beyond the pale by most Bushwhackers.

While guerrillas operated under the rule of a single leader with one or two trusted captains, partisan ranger units tended to be larger and organized more or less along military lines. Unlike guerrilla captains, who tended to be working men or from the middle

Dave Poole and two others of Quantrill's guerrillas, well supplied with pistols and a bottle of liquor, pose for a photograph while wintering in Texas. The drunken Bushwhackers did not like this picture and proceeded to destroy the photographer's equipment. Quantrill forced them to pay damages, but even this light taste of discipline was too much for the unruly guerrillas, and contributed to the breakup of Quantrill's command. (Courtesy State Historical Society of Missouri)

class, many leading partisans and cavalry raiders came from the wealthy elite. Nathan Bedford Forrest was a self-made millionaire, while Morgan inherited a prosperous business; Mosby was a successful lawyer, and Shelby and Porter were both wealthy landowners. Being from the cream of Southern society lent their organizations an air of chivalry that the guerrillas lacked. Most of these leaders looked at war in old-fashioned terms of honor and glory, thereby capturing the imagination of the Southern press. Forrest, the self-made man, was made of rougher stuff and commanded his men accordingly. A member of the 7th Tennessee Cavalry remembered: "When our movement was too slow to suit Forrest, he would curse, then praise, and then threaten to shoot us himself if we were so afraid the Yanks might hit us."

Partisan ranger leaders had the advantage of being able to handpick their men. Mosby in particular was careful whom he chose, turning away deserters and others he thought unreliable. Since his command acted in small detachments he needed men capable of independent thought; many came from the upper classes, or had prior military experience or special skills. His close relationship with J.E.B. Stuart meant that he had his pick from among Stuart's experienced cavalrymen, while guerrillas generally took whoever came along (although Quantrill turned away Jesse James for being too young.)

Both types of leader had a major advantage over officers in the regular army – they could distribute captured booty to their men. Theoretically partisan rangers had to sell arms and mounts to the Confederate Quartermaster at market value, while keeping enough to equip themselves, but otherwise they were free to take what they liked. The more honorable leaders forbade the outright robbery of civilians – Mosby strove to protect Unionist civilians in his territory – but joining a partisan ranger group offered the chance for considerable financial gain. On the famous "Greenback Raid" of October 13, 1864, Mosby's men stopped a passenger express out of Baltimore and netted $168,000 from the cash box, which was quickly divided among the 80 men present. Guerrillas took robbery to even greater extremes, and the motivation of many of them – especially in the Ozarks, Appalachians, and Louisiana bayou – seems to have been primarily financial.

CLOTHING AND WEAPONS: GUERRILLAS

Rebel guerrillas almost never wore Confederate uniforms. If they wore any uniform at all, they preferred captured Union ones, which allowed them to get the jump on Union soldiers or move in close to towns and depots unchallenged. As a countermeasure, local Union commanders created an elaborate set of hand signals to identify blue-clad men from a distance. An example from the Central District of Missouri instructed:

> The following signals and pass words for July, 1864, will be transmitted by sub-district commanders to the commanding officer of each scout, detachment, or escort detailed from their respective commands, every precaution being taken to prevent their being known to unauthorized persons:
>
> During the daytime the commanding officer of a scout, detachment, or escort, upon observing the approach of a party or body of men, will ride a few paces in advance of his command and raising his hat or cap, with arm extended at full height, will lower it slowly and place it upon his head. The commanding officer of the party thus challenged will immediately answer the same by raising the hat or cap from the head and extending the arm horizontally, bringing the arm back slowly and replacing the hat or cap upon the head. The signal to be given and answered, where the nature of the ground will permit, before the parties have approached nearer than from 300 to 350 yards.
>
> At night the party who first discovers the approach of another, when within challenging distance, will cry out loud and distinctly, "Halt!" and the party thus challenged will immediately answer, "Lyon," to be followed by a counter challenge of "Who comes there?" to which the party last challenged will answer "Reno." The failure of either party to answer promptly and correctly will be the signal to commence firing.

The badges to be worn during the month of July will be as follows: on the odd days, as the 1st, 3rd, 5th, 7th, &c., a red strip of cloth fastened around the hat or cap, and on the even days of the month, as the 2nd, 4th, 6th, 8th, &c., a white strip will be worn in the same manner, the colors alternating each day. Special care will be taken to avoid mishaps through negligence or the failure on the part of the men to change the badges as herein directed.

Despite such elaborate precautions, guerrillas often discovered the signals thanks to observant civilians or Confederate sympathizers serving in the militia.

When not wearing Union blue, Missouri Bushwhackers favored a peculiar piece of clothing called the "guerrilla shirt," a variation of the coat worn by hunters on the Great Plains. It was a pullover item open, sometimes deeply, down the front. Four large pockets, two in the breast and two on the sides, were big enough to hold cartridges, preloaded spare revolver cylinders or even small pistols. They came in a variety of colors, and the shawl-collar front, cuffs and pockets were often decorated with elaborate ribbonwork and needlework by a female relative or sweetheart. The Bushwhackers favored wide-brimmed slouch hats ranging in color from buff to dark brown and black, and often wore their hair shoulder-length. The guerrilla's whole ensemble was meant to create the image of a jaunty, brave, independent cavalier.

Fashion aside, what made the greatest impression was the small arsenal carried by Bushwhackers. Each armed himself with revolvers carried on a gunbelt, in pockets and saddle holsters; some carried as many as six, and their instant firepower against soldiers carrying single-shot, muzzle-loading rifle-muskets gave them a considerable edge. The favorite pistol was the Colt, especially the lighter .36cal Colt Navy, which was considered better for firing from horseback. A Bowie knife or even a tomahawk would be carried for hand-to-hand fighting. The favorite longarm was the breech-loading .52cal Sharps rifle, both for its accuracy and its speed in reloading; a trained marksman could fire this rifle up to ten times a minute. It had a maximum range of 800 yards and an effective range of about half that. Because the Sharps was a breech-loader, it could be reloaded while on horseback or lying down – a clumsy task with a standard muzzle-loader. A carbine version was also produced for cavalry work.

Not all guerrillas went into battle so well armed. In poorer areas such as western Virginia, Louisiana, or the Ozarks, they might be armed only with a shotgun or captured musket. Not surprisingly, these groups tended to avoid fights with large detachments of Federals, preferring to ambush stragglers or loot civilians. Because this meant fewer opportunities to capture weapons, they stayed poorly armed and peripheral to the main struggle.

Jayhawkers sometimes sported Union uniforms in an attempt to suggest official sanction for their actions, but most wore civilian clothing. Jennison's Kansas "Redlegs" got their name from their distinctive red pants, which served as a sort of uniform. Their choice of weapons was similar to that of Rebel guerrillas, although they were more likely to get Union equipment from the Quartermaster's department.

Both sides were generally well mounted, having ample opportunity to acquire the best horses from the civilian population.

Guerrillas fascinated period artists with their fierce appearance and even fiercer reputation. Here one is shown in tattered clothing armed with a musket and saber. The drawing is titled both "a jerilla" and "a deserter," reflecting the fact that they were often both. (LoC)

PARTISAN RANGERS

Due to their official status as members of the Confederate Army, partisan rangers usually wore standard cavalry uniforms – often with sweeping ostrich-feather hat plumes – but they were not above dressing in civilian clothing or Union uniforms to trick the enemy. Partisan commanders disagreed over the advisability of this, as anyone captured behind enemy lines not wearing Confederate uniform might be subject to summary execution. (Captured Union clothing was, of course, often pressed into service by Confederate troops of all kinds out of simple necessity.)

The weapons favored were the same as those of the guerrillas. The cavalry saber, standard issue among cavalry units, was almost universally abandoned because it weighed down the mount, took up space, and rarely got used; Morgan and his men considered the saber "as useless as a fence post." Revolvers were much more effective in hand-to-hand combat, as Forrest's men proved on numerous occasions when they decimated Union infantry who tried to fight them with bayonets. Partisan rangers relied on swift steeds to bypass superior forces and strike deep within enemy territory, but in battle some units dismounted and fought on foot. Morgan's 2nd Kentucky were known for this tactic, carrying regular rifles rather than cavalry carbines for their greater range. Many partisans, especially smaller groups in the Western and Trans-Mississippi theaters whose activities were limited to hit-and-run skirmishes, preferred the lighter carbines because they could be fired from horseback.

Both Southern guerrillas and partisan rangers captured a variety of weapons from the Union army, some of which had to be discarded for lack of ammunition. Confederate munitions works could never meet demand for even standard-issue weapons, and could not manufacture, for instance, the brass cartridges for the Spencer repeating carbine. Several accounts speak of partisans regretfully leaving these behind for lack of ammunition.

Cavalry commanders were divided on the usefulness of artillery. It could be of great benefit, as when Union Col Edward Hatch, commanding a detachment during Col Benjamin Grierson's 1863 Mississippi raid, dispersed a numerically superior force with the use of a single Woodruff 2-pdr, or when Capt John Morton's battery arrived just at the right moment to help Forrest break the Union line at Brice's Crossroads. Artillery was vital for destroying blockhouses and other fortifications. Morgan once tried to assault a blockhouse without artillery support and was repulsed with heavy losses; after that he made sure to take cannon on all his raids. But artillery could seldom keep pace with cavalry, and to keep the column from being slowed down too much only light pieces such as 6-pdrs would be used. Since the main purpose of raids was to destroy property rather than fight soldiers, cannon were seen as a supplemental rather than an essential tool.

TACTICS

Guerrillas and antiguerrillas

Guerrillas varied widely in their tactical ability. Most contented themselves with harassing civilians and sniping at small groups of enemy soldiers, while others developed a keen sense of tactics equal to that of any career officer.

The classic "bushwhack" was a simple yet effective ambush. One or more guerrillas concealed themselves in the undergrowth along a road, cutting a small hole in the greenery in the opposite direction from which the enemy would come; after the enemy passed, the guerrillas fired into their backs before slipping away. This forced Union troops to start patrolling in larger detachments, which used up manpower and limited the number of patrols. Troops crossing rivers at fords or on boats found themselves fired upon from the far bank, and the guerrillas would be long gone by the time the soldiers reached their position.

Guerrilla bands were especially effective at disrupting communications. Telegraph lines made easy targets, as did mail couriers, and in the worst areas entire companies had to escort a single courier. Exasperated Union officials sometimes forced known secessionist civilians to carry the mail, but this just encouraged them to join the guerrillas: they reasoned that if they were going to be shot at, they might as well be shot at by the enemy and not their own side. While couriers could be protected, the hundreds of miles of telegraph lines could not, and Union commanders had to resort to threats. The line from Springfield, Missouri, to Fort Smith, Arkansas, spent as much time down as up, so BrigGen John McNeil warned that he would hang a captured Bushwhacker wherever the line was cut, and the nearest house within ten miles would be burned if owned by a rebel sympathizer. Nor was river traffic safe from the guerrillas, who would snipe from the heavily forested riverbanks, forcing captains to add armor to their steamboats. If the guerrillas were lucky they might capture a boat as it lay moored at one of the many small river towns, stripping it of any supplies before sinking it.

While guerrillas often enjoyed superior firepower, the superior discipline of Federal troops usually carried the day if they got into an extended fight, and there are reports of the guerrillas retreating in the face of saber- and bayonet-charges. The rule among the guerrillas was to close quickly to bring their pistols to bear, and withdraw if they began taking serious casualties. It took some time for Union forces to wake up to the danger of guerrilla warfare, however. A year into the war, LtCol James Buel was supposed to be guarding Independence, one of the largest towns in western Missouri. He and his officers were billeted in various houses, while his troops had an unfortified camp on the outskirts of town. Despite the fact that the guerrillas raised a rebel flag in full view of the town Buel did nothing to concentrate his scattered troops, and was surprised by an early morning attack that wiped out his entire command.

Union officers in Missouri began to respond during the summer of 1862, when guerrillas had revealed a weakness during several failed attempts to take fortified buildings. Most western towns had a large brick courthouse in the middle of a wide square at the center of town; filling its windows with

D **DEFENDING A COURTHOUSE**
Many Union garrisons discovered that the safest place in town was the courthouse, which tended to be a large brick structure in the center of an open square; the door could be barricaded and the widows fortified with logs or sandbags. Without artillery, it was very difficult to take such a building by storm.
1: In this imagined but oft-repeated scenario, Confederate guerrillas wearing Union uniforms get to the edge of town without being challenged. They open fire on the scattered Union sentries and anyone else bearing arms. As they ride around the streets firing into the air to intimidate the populace, Union soldiers retreat to the fortified courthouse, which has already been well stocked with rifles and ammunition.

2: The guerrillas surround the courthouse square and snipe at the garrison from windows and doorways.
3: One group try to rush the courthouse to either torch it or storm their way inside, but the defenders – knowing that they will not be treated as prisoners-of-war – refuse to surrender and drive off the attack.
4 & 5: The frustrated guerrillas loot and burn stores, before riding off and disappearing into densely wooded country.

While courthouses proved difficult to take, their defenders could do little to help the inhabitants of the town. Guerrillas joked that the soldiers owned the courthouse, but they owned everything else.

logs and sandbags made an instant fort with a commanding field of fire, virtually invulnerable to an attacking force that lacked cannon.

Union timber blockhouses usually proved equally resistant; yet the guerrillas often boasted that while the Yanks controlled the towns, they controlled everything else. Guerrillas tended to be locals who knew the best hideouts, the best places for ambush and all the back roads, and they could rely on friends and neighbors to supply and inform them. Union troops, on the other hand, were often from other states and had to rely on vague maps and local guides of dubious loyalty. The guerrillas rode the best horses they could steal, or fine steeds given to them by sympathetic locals. The Union troops, especially local militias, were indifferently mounted on government-issue horses or even mules, and could often be outrun and outmaneuvered.

The key was to remain unnoticed, and guerrillas would often camp deep in the woods or create special shelters. John McCorkle, a scout for Quantrill, related: "We then dug a pit or cave in the side of the hill and covered it with logs, old boards and brush, with a fireplace in the back with a chimney made of sticks and mud. This was a warm place to stay, but we cooked only at night for fear the Federals would locate us by the smoke from the camp." McCorkle went on to describe one of their secret rendezvous, which they called "the bull-pen":

This was situated in the dense woods about a mile from Cedar Creek. There were two ways of approaching the "bull-pen," one through the bottom and the other through the woods south of John Moore's farm. We never approached this camp together, nor left it together, always going separately in different directions, in this way leaving no trail and this camp never was discovered by the Federals until after the war.

After guerrillas started sniping at river traffic, gunboats became essential for Union control of the waterways. The *Fort Hindman* was part of the Mississippi river fleet, and served in the Red River campaign; this civilian side-paddle steamer was converted for military use by the addition of iron plating and cannon, but even near the end of the war many boats were still armored with heavy timbers or even bales of cotton, as the need for gunboats far outstripped their production. Even iron plate could not protect them against cavalry raiders with artillery, or guerrillas who were lucky enough to pounce on them while they were moored; a number of boats changed hands more than once during the war. (LoC)

36

Since defensive measures only diverted guerrilla attacks to softer targets, the Federals had to try to hunt them down. Large cavalry sweeps achieved little except sending the guerrillas into temporary hiding, so in some areas the Union command created special antiguerrilla units. The 1st Arkansas Cavalry Volunteers, raised from Unionist Arkansans with a deep hatred for the guerrillas who had brought anarchy to their state, ruthlessly hunted down and killed more than 200 of them, more than any other unit in Arkansas. They kept on constant patrol, bringing along howitzers to cow an enemy unaccustomed to facing artillery. At times these units won pitched battles against concentrations of up to 1,000 guerrillas united to defeat them. Like Union troops in other states they burned the homes of secessionists, but they also targeted gristmills because these were used as meeting grounds and supply depots for the guerrillas.

Less successful was BrigGen Alfred Ellet's Mississippi Marine Brigade, formed to eliminate the guerrillas who constantly harassed Union shipping, thus increasing costs and slowing deliveries. These 1,200 men, provided with eight troop transports, several other boats and a battery of 6-pdrs, chugged up and down the river between Memphis, Tennessee, and Vicksburg, Mississippi, in 1863. They targeted spots from which boats had been fired upon, searched for guerrillas and burned down the homes of local civilians for supposedly aiding them (on at least one occasion a Rebel guerrilla staged his attacks from a Unionist town in order to get the wrong civilians punished.) Ellet's men lacked the discipline of the 1st Arkansas, and failed to do more than add to the region's misery.

Dr Charles Jennison, leader of the Kansas Redlegs and the most colorful of the Jayhawkers, shown here dressed as a hunter from the Great Plains. Hunting Missouri secessionist civilians and running off horses became his favorite pastimes, and he may have been the first Unionist to arm African Americans. He took part in the mass clearances and pillaging in western Missouri that followed Quantrill's Lawrence raid. (Kansas State Historical Society)

CENTRALIA & RAWLINGS LANE

"Bloody Bill" Anderson was one of the war's most competent guerrilla tacticians, whose most notorious exploit was the raid on Centralia, Missouri, on September 27, 1864 – an attack that exemplifies the daring and bloodthirstiness that were the key to the Bushwhackers' success in the Trans-Mississippi theater. Major-General Sterling Price had entered Missouri from Arkansas leading an army of 12,000 men, with the intention of taking St Louis. To soften up the state's defenses he had instructed Missouri Bushwhackers to harass Union garrisons and disrupt communications. Anderson received the order while camped with about 250 men at a secessionist farmer's house near the small railroad town of Centralia.

At dawn on September 27, Anderson and 30 men rode into the ungarrisoned village, whooping and shooting their pistols in the air to terrify the inhabitants into submission. Anderson wanted to read the St Louis newspapers for information on Price's movements, but his men soon started looting; several got drunk, and set fire to the depot. As Anderson's men ran wild, bursting into homes to demand breakfast and robbing people at gunpoint, a stagecoach drew into town. The passengers were all robbed, including US Representative James Rollins (the quick-thinking politician

Well-known death photo of "Bloody Bill" Anderson, propped up in a chair after being shot by a lucky Union militiaman. Anderson is posed with one of his Colt Navy revolvers in his right hand and another in the holster on his left side. He wears an elaborately embroidered "guerrilla shirt," an affectation of Trans-Mississippi Bushwhackers. (Courtesy State Historical Society of Missouri)

managed to convince the Bushwhackers that he was a secessionist preacher, but while they spared him they rifled through his valise and stole his silk shirt.) At noon the westbound train pulled in; the guerrillas, despite being drunk and scattered around town, immediately converged. A hastily erected barricade stopped the train and the Bushwhackers ordered all the passengers out. Among them were 25 unarmed Union soldiers on furlough; the Bushwhackers lined them up, took their uniforms, and Anderson asked if there were any officers among them. When Sgt Thomas Goodman meekly identified himself he was ordered out of line. Goodman thought he was a dead man, but to his surprise Anderson gave the order to kill the privates, preferring to keep Goodman to exchange for one of their number who had recently been

Irregular warfare required constant riding, quickly wearing out horses, and guerrillas and raiders routinely helped themselves to local stock in disputed territory. The civilian populations naturally saw this as theft; the original caption of this period engraving is "Guerrilla depredations." Raiders also often crept into the enemy's military camps to stampede their horses, slipping past or overpowering sentries and driving the horses through the sleeping camp, causing chaos and hampering pursuit. (LoC)

captured. The Bushwhackers then set fire to the train, tied up Goodman, and set off to rejoin their main group back at camp, but not before filling up looted boots with stolen whiskey.

At 4pm, Maj A.V.E. Johnston led 158 mounted riflemen from the Union 39th Missouri Infantry into town, led by the smoke from the burning train. Despite being unsure of the enemy numbers Johnston divided his force in two, leaving a small group to guard the town while he led the others in pursuit. When Anderson became aware of them he wiped them out in a carefully prepared ambush (detailed in Plate B), before galloping back into Centralia and killing the rest of Johnston's men. The Bushwhackers then disappeared into the thick woods of Howard County, and the trail was stone cold before Union troops gathered in sufficient strength to dare to patrol the area. Raids by Anderson's and other irregulars helped Price's campaign by drawing off troops that could have been used against his army. They disrupted mail, stalled riverboat service, and cut miles of telegraph wires, thus hampering the ability of far-flung Union militias to coordinate their actions.

Another incident shows Anderson's use of terrain. Learning on August 28, 1864, that Capt Joseph Parke with 44 men of the 4th Missouri State Militia Cavalry was searching for him, Anderson rode his entire command of a few dozen men down Rawlings Lane, a dead-end road with a heavy rail fence on either side. Satisfied that they had made a clear trail in the dirt, they jumped the north fence and doubled back to the western entrance of Rawlings Lane, where they hid behind a hill. Anderson sent 12 well-mounted men to fire upon the militia and retreat down Rawlings Lane as if in confusion; Parke, thinking he had routed the tail end of Anderson's main force, obediently chased them down the lane, and as soon as he had passed, Anderson charged his rear. Finding themselves trapped, the militiamen panicked, and Parke himself abandoned his men as they retreated in disorder. Eight were killed in the lane, and six more in a running fight stretching over 5 miles to Sulphur Springs, where the militiamen took refuge behind the walls of a deserted house. Not wanting to turn his victory into defeat by attacking a protected position, Anderson drew off.

PARTISAN RANGERS AND CAVALRY RAIDERS

A combination of mobility, disinformation campaigns, knowledge of terrain, and aggressiveness were the keys to success for partisan rangers and cavalry raiders alike.

Partisan rangers used many of the same tactics as guerrillas, but since they generally constituted larger forces they also employed small-scale battle tactics. Their adversaries tended to outnumber them, so partisans only gave battle at a time and place of their own choosing. Most bands avoided direct fights with equal or greater forces, yet fought smaller detachments as often as was practicable, because a high degree of activity behind Federal lines drew Union forces away from the main campaigns.

Colonel Joseph C. Porter of Missouri suffered for failing to follow this practice. His force, which rarely numbered more than a couple of hundred, was too small and ill-trained to sustain constant campaigning. As he recruited in northern Missouri in the summer of 1862 his numbers swelled to 2,000, but they were mostly unarmed farmers who he wanted to get south to Arkansas so they could join the Confederate army. Union forces ran his band to ground in a series of engagements that decimated and scattered it.

An important weapon in the partisan's arsenal was misinformation, often with the aid of sympathetic civilians. "Swamp Fox" Thompson liked to spread the rumor that he planned to attack a fort when he was really leaving the area; with the Union troops barricaded inside awaiting an attack, he could move away unmolested. Other leaders used civilians to exaggerate their numbers to local Union militia to discourage them from attacking; conversely, if they wanted to fight they would have their civilian helpers play down their numbers to give Union soldiers a false sense of security. Morgan had an even better resource: George "Lightning" Ellsworth, a telegraph operator who tapped into Union lines and was so skilled that he could imitate the distinctive "fist" of individual Federal operators (see Plate E). After listening in for a time to discover Union plans, he would then send fake orders and reports, or reroute trains of reinforcements out of harm's way.

Partisan rangers survived because they remained constantly on the move. Such long rides were exceedingly wearing on the men, who would tie themselves to the saddle and sleep in relays, with others making sure they did not drop out of line (horses will generally follow other horses, but a sleeping rider can unconsciously pull on the reins and make the horse stop or move away.) Partisans took care to avoid being tracked, and crossing heavily-patrolled railroads posed special hazards. Horsemen usually crossed the track singly, spaced at least 40 feet apart along its length so that their

An impression of Mosby's men keeping a rendezvous at the Blue Ridge pass, Shenandoah Valley. With their intimate knowledge of the land, raiders could scatter and regroup in rough terrain under cover of darkness, when regular Union troops risked getting disorganized, lost, or ambushed. (LoC)

hoofprints were less noticeable and, even if seen, might be mistaken for farmers or stray horses rather than a large body of men. Another trick, used when riding through the woods and needing to cross a dirt road, was to lay blankets across it first to prevent leaving a clear trail. If the Union presence grew too strong the commander of a small local partisan company might disband, sending each man home until called up again; some individuals acted as guerrillas in the meantime.

Partisans generally operated in small mounted detachments, and while Mosby commanded more men he usually split his command into groups of not more than 30 men led by a trusted officer, each group with a specific goal. This was especially suited to western Virginia, which had densely wooded hills and mountains offering easy shelter but also good roads, making travel easy. The Union army had been fighting guerrillas in Mosby's area of operations for two years before he arrived; constant attacks on the railroad had forced the Federals to construct blockhouses at key bridges and stations, and provide armored rolling-stock to protect trains and work-crews. These worked well against untrained guerrillas, but Mosby's expert intelligence-gathering found gaps in the defenses. The Union could not afford to armor all the trains, and Mosby could always find a stretch of defenseless track or an unwary patrol to pounce upon.

As in Arkansas and Missouri, Union commanders in western and northern Virginia took their frustration out on the local populace, burning homes and even executing suspected informants. The destruction reached its peak during Gen Philip Sheridan's 1864 Shenandoah campaign when, after pushing Jubal Early out of the Valley, Sheridan pulled back north, burning everything as he went. While historians have often said this was to deny Lee's Army of Northern Virginia food supplies, Sheridan's own stated purpose was to destroy the guerrillas' means of subsistence. This had failed in Arkansas, and it failed here; enraged guerrillas redoubled their efforts, joined by civilians who now had nothing to lose.

A relatively successful measure was the creation of specialized counterinsurgency units along the lines of the 1st Arkansas Cavalry, the best of which was Capt Richard Blazer's Independent Scouts. This small unit of elite troopers, armed with seven-shot Spencer repeaters, spent much of 1864 chasing Mosby. They treated civilians and prisoners leniently to gain their

E TAPPING INTO THE TELEGRAPH LINE

Confederate BrigGen John Hunt Morgan's most valuable raider was probably a Canadian named George "Lightning" Ellsworth, who expertly tapped into Union telegraph lines. This not only allowed him to pick up Union message traffic, but also to send deceptive messages exaggerating Morgan's numbers, giving false reports of his movements, and even creating phantom armies. Each telegraph operator had a distinctive "fist," his own way of sending Morse code that others would recognize like an individual voice. Ellsworth was an expert at imitating them, thus fooling Union telegraph operators into thinking they were communicating with colleagues they had known for years. One explanation for "Lightning's" nickname was that he once did his wiretapping trick during a thunderstorm, and miraculously avoided getting struck by lightning.

1: Ellsworth is shown wearing civilian clothing and boots fitted with logger's crampons to help him climb the pole. The portable hand telegraph key was used by both armies; here Ellsworth is employing the simplest method, hooking a wire from a terminal of his key to the uninsulated cable, with a second wire from the other terminal acting as a ground (earth.) More secure results were obtained by using both wires from the key to bridge across a cut in the cable.

2: BrigGen Morgan, and

3: his brother-in-law, Col Basil Duke, wear typical uniforms of Confederate cavalry officers; black ostrich-feather hat plumes were extremely popular. They carry Colt Navy revolvers, considered by Morgan to be far more useful than cavalry carbines, though his men also carried rifle-muskets so that they could fight as infantry.

confidence, and often wore Confederate uniforms or civilian clothing; in sum, they acted like the partisans they sought to defeat. Mosby found Blazer a continual thorn in his side, losing many men to his attacks, until one of his officers finally surprised Blazer's camp. Mosby's men outnumbered Blazer's two-to-one, and closed in quickly before the Federals' repeaters could be brought to bear. Blazer's command was destroyed and he himself was taken prisoner, but his success led to the creation of more counterinsurgency units.

In the Western theater, Morgan and Forrest worked in larger groups to conduct major raids. Morgan preferred to gain the enemy's rear as quickly as possible in order to avoid getting bogged down in fights with numerous combat-ready frontline troops. He would then send detachments out to his flanks to burn bridges and wreck rails to slow pursuit; these groups avoided large enemy groups or any fortification that withstood an initial artillery bombardment. The main body would then hit the prime objective, and the entire force would retreat to friendly lines, avoiding any engagement for fear of being slowed down. John McNeill had a similar philosophy for his much smaller force, summed up simply as "find a way out before going in." Forrest had a liking for double-envelopment attacks, his best being at Brice's Crossroads (detailed in Plates F & G). While Morgan often avoided fights for the sake of speed, Forrest preferred to keep his troopers constantly fighting detachments and outposts, to "keep up the skeer." His most famous line – "get there first with the most men" – summed up standard operating procedure among cavalry raiders, although few perfected it as he did.

Raiders usually sent scouts in civilian clothing out in advance to check road conditions, river levels, and troop dispositions. On the march the scouts would stay several miles ahead of the army, with one or two companies riding as advance guard about half a mile ahead of the main body. Then came the main force, with any wagons or artillery in the center to protect them and keep them accessible; flankers and a strong rearguard completed the marching order. The rate of march averaged about 3mph, with a break of about ten minutes per hour if the situation permitted. The gait would often be changed from trot to canter or even short gallops in order to keep the horses from getting worn down by repetitive motion.

While the most famous raiders were on the Confederate side, the Union eventually learned to imitate their tactics. In April 1863, Col Benjamin Grierson supported Grant's advance on Vicksburg by raiding with 1,700 troopers through Mississippi, starting from Tennessee and ending up in Union-held Baton Rouge, Louisiana. His main objective was Mississippi's railroads, critical to supplying Vicksburg. To elude pursuit he sent numerous detachments to wreak havoc in various directions, so confusing Mississippi's Home Guard that by the end of the raid the Confederate command simply had no idea where Grierson was or how many men he had. Like many of his Rebel counterparts, Grierson was not averse to dressing his scouts in civilian clothing or enemy uniforms. By far the largest cavalry raid of the war was a Union operation, when in the spring of 1865 the 27-year-old MajGen James Wilson led an entire cavalry corps of almost 14,000 men through northern Alabama and into Georgia, destroying industry in this previously untouched region. Wilson outmaneuvered and outfought Nathan Bedford Forrest and captured the fleeing President Jefferson Davis; his success was largely due to imitating Forrest in having a mobile force unencumbered by a large wagon train, and carrying serious firepower – in his case, Spencer repeaters.

Partisan rangers varied their activities depending on the local terrain. Two bands operating on the Mississippi near Memphis, Tennessee, led by Capts James McGhee and Joseph Barton, were composed mainly of boatmen, and specialized in attacking Union shipping. In early 1863 McGhee's group captured and burned three steamers and sank 12 coal barges, and their attack on the

Hit-and-run tactics were not always successful. A quick and determined counterattack, or an effective pursuit by well-mounted cavalry, could turn the tables, and if the raiders took too much booty with them they were as encumbered as regular soldiers. (*Frank Leslie's Illustrated Newspaper*)

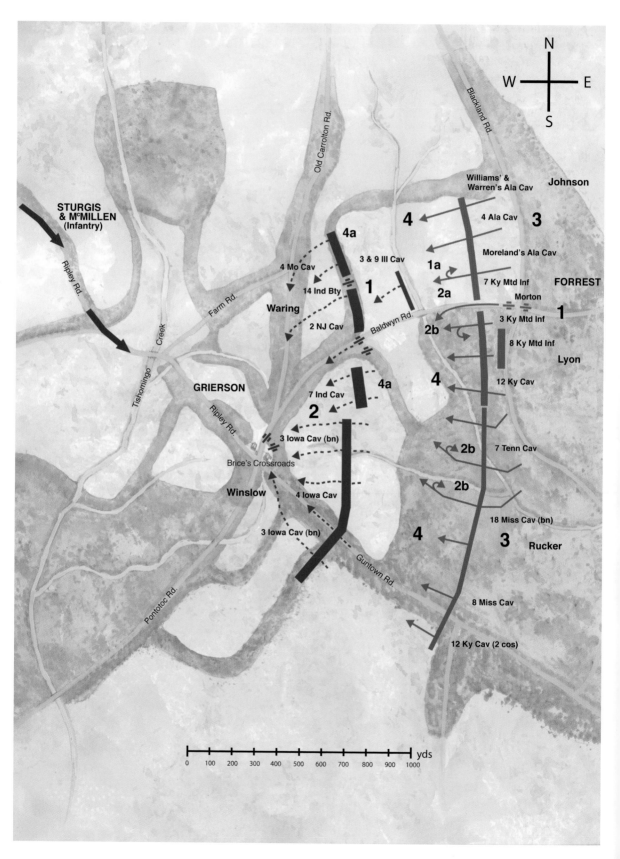

steamer *Jacob Musselman* on January 6 was typical. As the boat pulled into the landing at Hopefield, ten of McGhee's men stormed aboard. They ordered the boat upriver several miles to where the rest of the band were waiting; the partisans stripped it of everything of value, used it to capture a passing flatboat filled with livestock, and then burned both boats. (The Union response was also typical: the commander at Memphis, MajGen Stephen Hurlbut, ordered Hopefield burned for giving aid and shelter to the "guerrillas.")

Brigadier-General Meriwether J. Thompson, dubbed the "Swamp Fox" for his constant marching and countermarching through the supposedly impassable swamps of southeast Missouri, kept Union commanders guessing by sending spare horses to one place, and the bulk of his men to a different spot where he had stored boats. His force would hit the enemy, go to the boats, and cross a swamp to where the horses waited. This led his opponents to exaggerate his strength, and frustrated them because they could never catch him. One Union soldier complained: "He seems always to be doin' the runnin', but the other fellow's the one that's gettin' shot."

THE IMPACT OF IRREGULAR WARFARE

GUERRILLAS AND THE CIVILIAN POPULATIONS

No guerrilla force can survive for long without the active support of at least a part of the civilian population, on whom they rely for food, information, and

F BATTLE OF BRICE'S CROSSROADS, JUNE 10, 1864

This was a prime example of the employment of large numbers of partisan rangers in a pitched battle. Concerned about MajGen Nathan Bedford Forrest's regular attacks on the Nashville & Chattanooga Railroad in Tennessee, Gen Sherman ordered BrigGen Samuel Sturgis into northern Mississippi to distract and hopefully defeat Forrest while Sherman made an advance into Georgia. Sturgis had 5,200 infantry, 3,300 cavalry, 22 cannon and 200 wagons. Forrest commanded 4,900 veteran cavalry.

On June 10, 1864, Forrest decided to attack Sturgis at Brice's Crossroads about 15 miles east of Tupelo. Forrest knew the Union cavalry rode far ahead of their infantry; the muddy roads would hamper infantry movement, and since that day dawned hot the infantry would be tired out before they got into the fight. Tishomingo Creek lay not far to the west, crossed by a single bridge, and patches of thick woodland would screen his movements. Forrest intended to defeat Sturgis in detail, first beating his cavalry and then his infantry.

BEATING THE CAVALRY, 10am – 1pm

1: The Union vanguard of 1,500 cavalry under Grierson arrived at Brice's Crossroads at 9.30am, and a Union patrol a mile east along the Baldwyn Road skirmished with Forrest's 7th Kentucky vanguard before withdrawing to the main body. The Union 3rd and 9th Illinois and 2nd New Jersey cavalry halted at the edge of an open field a half-mile east of the crossroads on either side of Baldwyn Road, and formed up behind a rail fence backed by trees.

1a: Forrest's 1,300 strong vanguard – 3rd, 7th and 8th Kentucky – formed up a quarter-mile away on the other side of the field. The Confederates charged at 10am, but were repulsed – note that the cavalry of both sides fought dismounted, with horse-holders to the rear.

2: As the Union vanguard sent word back for the infantry to hurry up, the rest of the Union cavalry arrived, making a wide arc of 3,300 dismounted troopers, with four howitzers, astride the Baldwyn Road.

2a & 2b: From 10.45am, Forrest attacked the Union center twice more while his reinforcements began to arrive, being driven back but keeping the Union troops on the defensive.

3: From 11am, the arrival of Confederate reinforcements increased Forrest's strength to 2,100 and extended the Rebel flanks, with the 4th Alabama on the right wing and the 7th Tennessee, 18th and 8th Mississippi south to the Guntown Road.

4 & 4a: At about noon, Forrest ordered an all-out attack along his entire line. The Union right center and left flank broke, forcing the whole Union line to fall back shortly before 1pm. The Union cavalry crowded back to about a quarter-mile east of the crossroads. Simultaneously, the Union infantry began to arrive, to find ambulances and horses jamming the crossroads and cavalrymen falling back in disorder. The troopers were exhausted, nearly out of ammunition, and demoralized, and the infantry quickly moved up to take their place in a shortened front line. Forrest now held the fenced field between the Old Carrolton and Baldwyn roads. (Continued on page 50)

sometimes shelter. In bad weather guerrillas often lodged at the homes of sympathizers, but this could be perilous. Arkansas guerrilla Joseph Bailey noted in his memoirs: "I preferred the shadows of the deep woods to the shelter of a house, regardless of the weather. A house was liable to be surrounded or waylaid at any time, and many lives were lost in that way...". Both Anderson and Quantrill had to fight their way out of several such situations; Quantrill never learned his lesson, and was killed when he was tracked down to a secessionist farm in Kentucky.

In some areas civilians developed an elaborate network of guides and spies, usually old men and even women who would draw less suspicion. Each guide would be responsible for only a short stage of a rapid relay system so that they would not attract attention by being too far from home. They identified each other through signs and passwords that changed regularly. The *Kansas City Journal* for 17 June 1862 complained: "Their spys [sic] may frequently be seen upon high points going through such gyrations as to leave no doubt that they have a perfect system of signals among them, by which the approach of troops is instantly communicated over a large tract of country."

Sometimes civilians helped fight, joining up for brief periods or sniping at Union troops on their own initiative. In one remarkable case, Capt Albert Peabody and 65 men of the 1st Missouri Cavalry surprised Quantrill's band camped at a farm. They managed to cut the guerrillas off from their horses, forcing Quantrill and his men to flee on foot. In the meantime, however, locals

The draft was widely unpopular on both sides, as this cartoon shows: a man has just had his wife cut off his finger, while another man assures him it won't hurt long and he'll soon get a medical certificate. Taking to the woods as a guerrilla was a much more popular way of avoiding conscription than self-mutilation. (LoC)

CANDIDATES FOR THE EXEMPT BRIGADE._

48

Heavy-handed brutality in Union-occupied areas sometimes led to spontaneous violence by local residents, as is recorded in this 1862 drawing in which a group of farmers fire on a pair of unsuspecting, and unarmed, Union soldiers. (LoC)

had begun to converge from the surrounding countryside; they fired on the Union troops, and Peabody found himself battling a hundred civilians. While this caused few Union casualties, it did give the Bushwhackers time to escape.

The other side of the coin was the considerable suffering that irregular warfare brought down on civilian populations. Guerrillas might treat civilians of either side harshly, and the chaos of war gave birth to countless gangs of deserters and bandits. The Ozarks, particularly, were rife with thieving bands, who tortured civilians indiscriminately to force them to reveal hidden money – burning their feet was a common method. (One Alf Bolin actually boasted that he had killed 30 Union men and an almost equal number of Confederates.)

Government countermeasures caused even more widespread hardships; those suspected of harboring guerrillas were shot or thrown into crowded and disease-ridden prisons, and in areas of high guerrilla activity numerous restrictions were placed on known secessionists. Their businesses were closed down or boycotted, and they were subject to searches, often being robbed in the process. In some areas they had to get permits to travel and were forced to take loyalty oaths, which usually included payment of a hefty bond. Expressing secessionist sympathies could lead to fines or imprisonment, and Union patrols lived off the land by plundering secessionist homes. Nor were the victims entirely secessionists; some dishonest officers took advantage of the situation to steal, and Unionist newspapers found themselves shut down if they criticized the way the government handled the war.

Union soldiers frequently tried to entrap civilians by showing up at their homes pretending to be guerrillas, and then trying to extract information about the whereabouts of real guerrillas or civilian sympathizers. Nor could civilians even be sure of the identity of men in blue; by the middle of the war many guerillas had Union uniforms, plundered from supply trains or stripped from dead bodies. Often guerrillas would show up at a homestead dressed in blue and question the residents about

Union troops dismantling a fence for firewood. Armies left a swath of destruction in their wake; while stealing a farmer's fence may seem minor compared to some depredations practiced by both sides, it meant considerable extra labor for the farmer and increased resentment against the occupying army. (LoC)

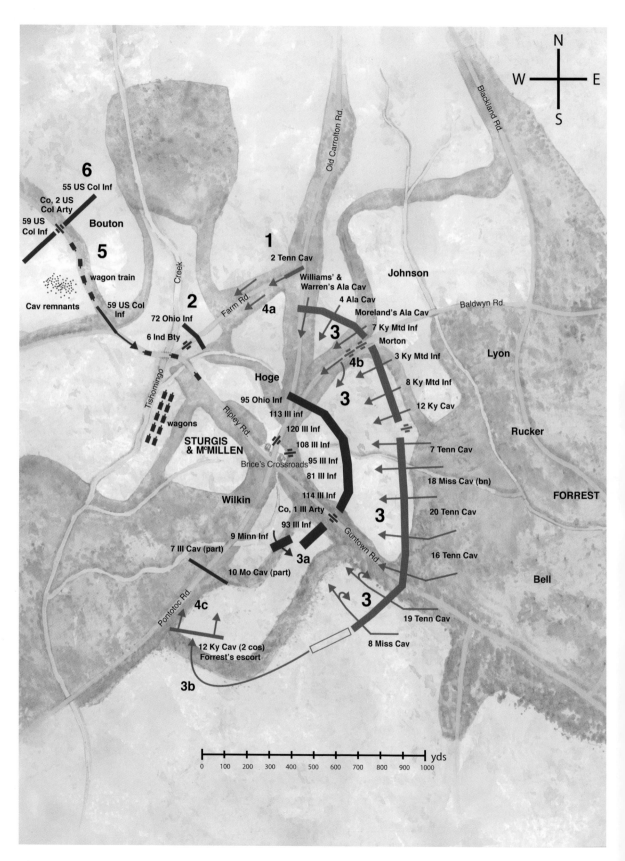

N
W   E
S

6
55 US Col Inf
Co, 2 US Col Arty
59 US Col Inf
Bouton

5
wagon train
Cav remnants
59 US Col Inf

Creek

2
72 Ohio Inf
6 Ind Bty

Tishomingo

wagons

STURGIS & McMILLEN

Brice's Crossroads

Ripley Rd.

Hoge

95 Ohio Inf
113 Ill inf
120 Ill Inf
108 Ill Inf
95 Ill Inf
81 Ill Inf
114 Ill Inf
Co, 1 Ill Arty
93 Ill Inf
9 Minn Inf

Wilkin

7 Ill Cav (part)
10 Mo Cav (part)

Pontotoc Rd.

4c

12 Ky Cav (2 cos)
Forrest's escort

3b

3a

Guntown Rd.

1
2 Tenn Cav
Williams' & Warren's Ala Cav

4a

Old Carrolton Rd.

Johnson

Baldwyn Rd.

4 Ala Cav
Moreland's Ala Cav
7 Ky Mtd Inf
Morton
3 Ky Mtd Inf
8 Ky Mtd Inf
12 Ky Cav

3

4b

3

Lyon

Rucker

7 Tenn Cav
18 Miss Cav (bn)
20 Tenn Cav
16 Tenn Cav

FORREST

3

Bell

19 Tenn Cav
8 Miss Cav

Blackland Rd.

yds
0 100 200 300 400 500 600 700 800 900 1000

their loyalties, facing them with the hideous dilemma of having to try to guess who they were talking to, at the risk of death if they guessed wrong. The wisest course for unwilling hosts to bands of armed men was to say as little as possible, cook them a good meal, and allow themselves to be robbed without resistance.

Union authorities imposed collective punishments to discourage attacks, fining local inhabitants when guerrillas destroyed railways or telegraph lines. When the town of Keytesville, Missouri, was attacked by Bushwhackers on September 20, 1864, the 35 militiamen cowering in the fortified courthouse surrendered without a fight and seven of them promptly joined the Rebels. The Bushwhackers plundered the town, burned the courthouse, and killed two local Unionists. In retaliation, the Union military government fined local secessionists $50,000 to pay damages to the families of the slain men and to build a new courthouse.

The Ozarks and Appalachians were especially hard hit. Entire counties became virtually depopulated as thousands of people fled to the safety of Union- or Confederate-controlled territory. Many families were burned out, their menfolk murdered and their crops and animals stolen. Ragged, hungry refugees gathered in the nearest cities and became a burden on the governments of both sides. In March 1865 almost as many rations were issued to refugees in Fort Smith, Van Buren, and Fayetteville, Arkansas, as were issued to Union

G BEATING THE INFANTRY, 1pm – 2.30pm

1: Some 2,800 more Rebel cavalry arrived; the 2nd, 16th, 19th and 20th Tennessee extended Forrest's arc on the left, while Morton's battery of eight cannon were set up in the field along the Baldwyn Road. The 2nd Tennessee were sent around the Union left to the Farm Road, to take the bridge over the Tishomingo.

2: There was a short pause while these deployments took place, and while Sturgis' and McMillen's Union infantry replaced the cavalry in the front line, which was now only about 300 yards east of Brice's Crossroads. The 72nd Ohio Infantry and two cannon from the 6th Indiana Battery were placed on a knoll on the Farm Road just east of the bridge.

3: Shortly after 1.30pm Forrest launched an all-out attack before most of the Union infantry could catch their breath. The fighting continued for an hour at close quarters, with the Confederate cavalrymen firing their pistols to great effect.

3a & 3b: A Union counterattack on the right by the 9th Minnesota forced back the 8th Mississipi and 19th Tennessee Cavalry, but Forrest sent his escort and part of the 12th Kentucky Cavalry around this flank.

4a: On the other wing, about 250 men of the 7th Tennessee Cavalry attacked down the Farm Road, widely deployed to conceal their small numbers and with the bugler repeating commands from different locations in the thick woods. The Union defenders repulsed them at about 2pm, but the attack caused panic.

4b: Meanwhile, in the center, Forrest's artillery came up to point-blank range, firing with double-shotted canister into densely packed Union infantry.

4c: On the Confederate far left, the 12th Kentucky and Forrest's escort swept around the Union right wing. All these events were more or less simultaneous. Consequently, the Union line contracted into an ever-smaller arc until it covered only about 300 yards around the crossroads, which became jammed with men who made easy targets but were unable to maneuver. Forrest, too, shortened and reinforced his battle line. Sturgis ordered a general withdrawal, and by 2.30pm Union troops were falling back in disorder up the Ripley Road and abandoning their cannon and other equipment.

5: The second part of the Union wagon train had halted along the Ripley Road west of the bridge, but other vehicles were jamming the road east of the Tishomingo and the crossroads itself.Some 1,200 US Colored Troops who had been accompanying the wagons reached a position near the bridge and covered the retreat as men poured across it, but a wagon overturned on the bridge, adding to the chaos and forcing many men to wade or swim – some drowned in the attempt. Meanwhile, the Confederate artillery moved to the crossroads and shelled the mass of retreating men, killing many. The Confederates charged the black troops and engaged in hand-to-hand combat, forcing them to join the retreat.

6: The pursuit continued to a ridge a half-mile west of the bridge, where the Union Colored Troops and remnants of other units formed a line, but this too was soon set running.

As darkness fell a detachment of Forrest's cavalry kept up the pressure while the rest looted the abandoned wagons. The rout continued into the next day as Forrest chased Sturgis' shattered army across six counties. The battle cost him 495 casualties, but Sturgis lost 2,610 killed, wounded, captured or missing, as well as most of his artillery and wagons. This tactical masterpiece made Forrest's reputation, and slowed the Union advance into Alabama and Mississippi – although Sherman did achieve his goal of keeping the railroad unmolested during his drive into Georgia.

troops. This mass exodus hurt the guerrillas in the long run because it undercut their potential base of support.

Civilians had little chance to strike back, since frequent thefts and confiscations by both armies had left most noncombatants without weapons. One of the only real ways to resist was to inform on other civilians, directing the guerrillas' wrath to another doorstep. Amid such widespread lawlessness it was not surprising that civilians often became part-time guerrillas themselves; as one Arkansas man put it, "It was war times and who cared for burning a house when the enemy burns yours?". In an attempt to stop the anarchy Col Marcus La Rue Harrison of the 1st Arkansas Cavalry (Union) created more than a dozen fortified "colonies." A Home Guard of 50 men would be armed and moved with their families to a defensible location, where they built an earthen fort or timber blockhouse. Each man got a parcel of land and regular supplies, and everyone within ten miles of a colony had to join or leave. The colonies helped deal with the refugee problem, denied guerrillas their best source of plunder, and acted as way-stations for patrols. A whole region of northwest Arkansas was denied to the guerrillas as a base of operations; soon the colony system spread throughout the state, and there was even one for freed slaves.

Often the only protection civilians could count on was the Federal army, and this helped to win over a large segment of the populace sick of a life of constant fear. The most lawless guerrillas would even kill Confederate government officials, especially conscription agents; even in Confederate-held areas the government had trouble running mail, raising taxes, enforcing the law, and maintaining other basic services. The end of the war came as a relief to many Southern sympathizers.

However, it must be stressed that the civilian experience of partisan rangers was entirely different. While partisans were not above taking what they needed, they generally did not otherwise molest noncombatants; "Mosby's Confederacy" afforded protection to civilians of either loyalty, essentially acting as a civilian government. During Morgan's raid into Kentucky, Indiana, and Ohio his men actually robbed more from Northern secessionist "Copperheads" than loyal Unionists. They considered these so-called Rebels living safely in the North as worse than Unionists, claiming loyalties that they did not have to suffer for.

GUERRILLAS AND THE REGULAR ARMIES

Many guerrillas actively aided the campaigns of the regular armies. Their local knowledge and contacts made them excellent scouts, and at times they joined regular forces to fight pitched battles. Even unruly figures such as Quantrill and Ferguson on the Confederate and Beaty on the Union side did this on numerous occasions.

Regular officers tended to take a dim view of guerrillas, who generally ignored orders even when they could be found and given them. Many guerrillas in the Trans-Mississippi theater would leave their areas of operation in the autumn, when the cover of foliage disappeared, and spend the winter resting in Texas. Brigadier-General Henry McCulloch, whose Northern Sub-District of Texas was a popular wintering spot, became frustrated with these hardened fighters avoiding military duty while getting drunk and shooting up local towns, and his office was flooded with reports of citizens being robbed and even killed. To be sure, not all guerrillas acted in this fashion, but many had become little better than bandits operating under the veneer of Confederate service.

One commander who never lost his respect for guerrillas was MajGen Sterling Price. In a notable incident during his 1864 invasion of Missouri, he met with "Bloody Bill" Anderson and his group. Noticing human scalps dangling from their saddles, he became enraged and ordered the men out of his sight. The Bushwhackers returned later, *sans* scalps, and presented Price with

Refugees driven from their homes in areas of heavy guerrilla activity became a major burden to both armies. The problem was especially acute in Missouri and Arkansas, where large swaths of the countryside were all but depopulated. (*Frank Leslie's Illustrated Newspaper*)

"Contrabands" – the term used in the North for all Southern blacks, whether runaways or free – were employed in large numbers by Union MajGen Herman Haupt's US Military Railroad Construction Corps. Here they are demonstrating, with ropes, hooks and heavy beam levers, a technique for popping rails off their ties and twisting them. Rails that were only bent could be repaired in the field surprisingly often, but those that were twisted had to be sent back to rolling mills. These workers wear civilian clothing, but some have US Army forage caps. (LoC)

a pair of silver-mounted revolvers. Price treated them to a laudatory speech and said if he had 50,000 such men he could hold Missouri forever. He then sent them off to destroy railroads to slow Union pursuit, and a detachment of Anderson's group stayed with Price's army as scouts and cavalry.

Confederate frustration with the guerrillas reached its height in the Trans-Mississippi. In southern Arkansas, the autumn of 1863 found Confederate forces distracted by an attempt to stop plundering by their own guerrillas. In a sweep through northern Arkansas in early 1864, BrigGen J.O. Shelby hoped to gather recruits behind Union lines in territory ruled by the guerrillas, most of whom were paroled Confederate prisoners or deserters. He was soon disappointed, finding them to be "Confederate soldiers in nothing save the name, robbers and jayhawkers [who] have vied with the Federals in plundering, devouring and wasting the subsistence of Loyal Southerners... the condition of the so-called Confederate forces here was horrible in the extreme. No organization, no concentration, no discipline, no law, no anything." By the last year of the war the remnants of the Arkansas Confederate army were so busy hunting self-styled guerrillas that they had little time for fighting Federals.

H   WRECKING THE SOUTHERN RAILROADS

There were several techniques for sabotaging tracks, depending on available time, equipment, and manpower. These were typically employed during cavalry raids such as that led by Union Colonel Benjamin H. Grierson into Tennessee, Mississippi, and Louisiana between April 17 and May 2, 1863.

1: If their numbers were sufficient, raiders would pry a rail loose, hammer it at one point to weaken it, and use a large group of men to bend it.

2: Pried-up rails would be put atop a large bonfire made of railroad ties and fence posts. The heat made the rails so malleable that, in time, they would bend under their own weight.

3: If time allowed, heat-softened rails could be bent around trees.

4: Rails might be loosened at two points with picks and crowbars, and a whole section, still spiked to its ties, would be pushed over into a stream or gully.

5: The most vulnerable points on a railroad were bridges, whose wooden trestle supports could be cut, set on fire, or blown down with charges inserted in holes drilled into the timbers at vital points. If they had the time raiders often preferred to chop through supports in order to avoid a telltale column of smoke, but burning obviously destroyed a bridge more completely.

During Grierson's Raid, his 1,700 cavalrymen rode 800 miles and destroyed long stretches of two railroad lines, as well as supplies and locomotives.

Home Guards patrolled local neighborhoods in both the North and South, hunting irregular forces and acting as police. Here a Southern Home Guard unit checks the passes of slaves near Vicksburg, Mississippi. (*Frank Leslie's Illustrated Newspaper*)

Louisiana faced a similar problem. The Union army controlled the portion of the state east of the Mississippi, and the swampland just to the west of the river was a no-go area full of irregulars. Confederate authorities in western Louisiana actually cooperated with Federal forces on several occasions to hunt down the worst gangs. This was an interesting reversal of their initial policy, when they had sent a troop of partisan rangers under Capt James McWaters to keep civilians in the borderland Lafourche district from trading sugar and cotton with Union-occupied New Orleans. McWaters arrested

The 9th Missouri State Militia Cavalry muster before departing on an antiguerrilla operation. Note the variety of uniforms, which include items of civilian clothing; local militia tended to be poorly trained and equipped. They sometimes fared well against guerrillas when they could manage to run them to ground, but they were no match for partisan rangers and cavalry raiders. (Courtesy State Historical Society of Missouri)

a prominent sugar planter for trading with the enemy, and also seized stagecoaches and boats coming from New Orleans. While such plundering had been a part of military strategy earlier in the war, it later got far out of hand and needed to be stopped.

In the first year of the war in western Virginia and eastern Tennessee, the Union army relied on Unionist irregulars to fight for these regions until they could move in. While the Union guerrillas' efforts failed in Tennessee they did draw Confederate troops away from other campaigns, and the guerrilla war in western Virginia helped keep that region out of the Confederacy.

While most army officers found guerrillas unsavory, they afforded more respect to partisan rangers because of their official status, better discipline, and closer ties to the chain of command. Throughout his career Mosby worked as Stuart's and Lee's eyes, ears, and swordarm behind Federal lines. He acted independently and often on his own initiative, but always with the wider strategy in mind. As the Confederate army fell back in the last year of the war Mosby's men became the Confederacy's only sizable force in northern Virginia. Forrest, too, was always conscious of the larger picture, and was actually more of a regular cavalry officer than a partisan, although his independent fighting style led to him being perceived as the latter. When a successful partisan strayed too far from the overall plan the consequences could be fatal – as already described, Morgan's daring thrust into Indiana and Ohio, contrary to orders, led to the destruction of his command.

Morgan was not the only partisan leader who passed freely between independent command and the structure of the regular army. In Missouri and Arkansas, "Swamp Fox" Thompson spent much of the war conducting independent raids but would concentrate his forces to fight pitched battles (he even served for a time as commander of several rams in the Confederacy's Mississippi fleet.) Larger groups of partisans often acted as mobile Confederate brigades, not simply as irregular forces aiding the main army.

THE EFFECTIVENESS OF IRREGULAR WARFARE

Since irregulars were predominantly used by the Confederacy, the obvious point is that they did not save the South from defeat, but a closer look reveals that they both helped and hindered the war effort.

Guerrilla warfare in the "Bleeding Kansas" era helped draw the United States into civil war, creating an atmosphere of bitter and divisive lawlessness that made descent into open warfare all the easier. In the eyes of African Americans the most significant contribution would be that of the Kansas Jayhawkers, who led hundreds, perhaps thousands of slaves to freedom in

Some raids were spur-of-the-moment actions by regular soldiers, such as this cattle raid in an 1864 drawing. The original accompanying text reads: "Genl Wade Hampden [sic] suddenly appeared at Coggins point in the rear of the army, on the James river, and carried off the entire beef supply, about 2500 head of cattle. The rebel soldiers were much inclined to joke with the pickets on the loss of their meat rations; the Union men, on the other hand, thanked them heartily for removing the tough remnants of herds that had been driven behind the army all summer and which were at once replaced by a fresh stock much fitter for the table." (LoC)

A Union foraging party returning from the countryside shortly after the capture of Baton Rouge, Louisiana, on May 7, 1862. The men had endured a long boat voyage and were eager for fresh food. They found easy pickings in the poorly defended region, but such conduct hurt them in the long run by turning local sympathy in favor of the guerrillas. (*Frank Leslie's Illustrated Newspaper*)

Kansas. Generally, however, Union guerrillas and partisans had less of an impact than their Rebel counterparts. Their greatest legacy was the creation of the state of West Virginia, which came into being in 1863 in Virginia's predominantly Unionist western hill country after a determined guerrilla campaign backed by political pressure.

Few of the Confederate guerrilla bands in any of the three theaters had any effect on the war's ultimate outcome, beyond lengthening it and adding greatly to its material and human cost. It is clear that it was guerrillas from Arkansas who were largely responsible for the failure of the Union campaigns to take Little Rock in 1862 and Camden in 1864. However, those in the Ozarks – and the Louisiana bayou country – generally achieved little other than creating lawless regions that required both sides to expend men and resources in order to protect civilians and fight groups that were often little better than bandits. While also adding to civilian misery, the Bushwhackers in Missouri were the elite of the Confederacy's guerrillas; they pinned down Union forces, keeping them from launching sufficiently large invasions into southern Arkansas, Louisiana, and Texas. Irregular warfare gave secessionist civilians in Union-occupied areas a chance to actively support the Confederacy, boosting their morale; but some guerrilla bands spread only suffering and chaos, and ultimately cost the South the support of many civilians.

The impact of the partisan rangers is more obvious. Mosby hampered Hooker's Army of the Potomac during the Chancellorsville campaign in 1863, and slowed his response later that year during the Gettysburg campaign. Forrest's brilliant victory at Brice's Crossroads did not stop Sherman's drive into Georgia, but it did slow the Union advance into Alabama and Mississippi. The necessity for the Union army to build blockhouses and devote large numbers of men to guarding towns, railroads, and supply depots had a definite effect on the

Union's ability to launch major offensives. An argument can be made that the daring exploits of Forrest, Mosby, Morgan, and other cavalry raiders were a wasted effort, having little overall impact while denying the regular Confederate army of some of its best horsemen. Nevertheless, it is undeniable that their raids gave the South reason for hope when most news was bad. Morale, both of the army and the civilian population, is as important a part of any war effort as generals and munitions, and it is in this area that the partisan rangers had perhaps their greatest impact.

AFTERMATH

In the months following the surrender of the main Confederate armies, many people ached to settle scores before the rule of law was reestablished. Some could not convince themselves that the war was over, and many guerrillas did not want to give up their freebooting ways. This was especially true in more remote regions such as western Texas, the Indian Territory, Missouri, and Arkansas, which for months after the war were awash with former guerrillas, deserters, and also marauding Indians. Rural areas even in more populous states remained hazardous, and the Union occupation had trouble clamping down on the hordes of armed and experienced fighters wandering through the region, looking for food and shelter and not afraid to rob or kill to get them.

Bridges were prize targets of irregular fighters, since their destruction halted train traffic for days or even weeks until they could be rebuilt. In regions such as western Virginia and Missouri, with rough terrain and numerous streams, the Union army had to reserve a large number of personnel to protect the many bridges. (LoC)

AT REST
BILLIE DeMINT JR.
AGED ABOUT 10 YEARS.
HUNG BY GUERRILLA BAND DUR-
ING CIVIL WAR NOV. 1863.BECAU-
SE HE WOULD NOT TELL WHERE
HIS FATHER WAS.ERECTED BY HIS
FRIENDS.

This Missouri gravestone stands as mute testimony to the savagery of guerrilla warfare. The killing of under-aged civilians was rare, but not unknown; in this case, however, genealogical research revealed that the boy was actually 17 years old at his death, not ten. Stories of guerrilla exploits and atrocities alike became exaggerated in local folklore. (Courtesy State Historical Society of Missouri)

The Union command offered amnesty to all but the most notorious Southern guerrillas if they surrendered, although with the proviso that they were not free from civil prosecution. Many took the offer, but a few holdouts – either through loyalty to the Cause or for fear of civilian courts – refused. A few others actively helped to track down fellow guerrillas and encourage them to surrender; the very fact that these intermediaries themselves were still alive convinced their comrades to come in. They returned to an uneasy peace; most had had their farms burned and families driven away, and there was always the fear of vengeance at the hands of the Unionists who had once been their victims. Union guerrillas had a rather easier prospect of settling into postwar life. The law considered them legitimate fighters, and only Southerners hated them. There were a few vengeance killings, but for the most part Union guerrillas and Jayhawkers re-entered civilian life with no more difficulty than that which always faces returning soldiers prone to what we now call "post-traumatic stress disorder."

On both sides, however, and particularly in the Border States, some discovered that their acquired skills of hit-and-run raiding, hiding out in the woods, and robbing stagecoaches, trains, and banks had provided excellent training for later criminal careers. The most notorious outlaws of the immediate postwar period – Cole Younger, his brothers, and Frank and Jesse James – were all former guerrillas. There is little evidence that they were persecuted after the war, but years of merciless combat under the tutelage of Quantrill and Anderson had hardened them.

As after any civil war, animosities continued to divide the populace long after the fighting stopped, and flared up again on more than one occasion.

Former Confederate officers organized the Ku Klux Klan in 1865 to keep control of the South in the hands of Southern whites by fighting both African Americans and Northern "carpetbaggers" moving to the South to invest and exploit. Assisted for a time by Nathan Bedford Forrest, the KKK soon took on many aspects of a guerrilla campaign, threatening people with death if they did not leave and destroying homes and businesses. They also killed or injured more than 2,000 blacks in Louisiana during the weeks leading up to the 1868 presidential election, to keep African Americans from exercising their new right to vote. Forrest and other members of the South's genteel society soon distanced themselves from the KKK, arguing that these attacks only made the occupation worse, and President Grant all but destroyed the first-generation Klan in the early 1870s.

The Civil War had allowed family and personal feuds to escalate to new levels of violence, and this bitterness was slow to heal. One of the last incidents that can be traced to the Civil War was the feud between the "Baldknobbers" and the "antiBaldknobbers" in the 1880s. In the Ozark hill country of southern Missouri, returning Confederates found that they had lost their farms for failure to pay taxes and that Unionists now owned their land. A new state constitution forbade former Confederates from voting; they soon formed an angry underclass, and tensions ignited into violence in 1883. Former Unionists founded the Baldknobber vigilante organization, so named because they met atop treeless hills called bald knobs where they could keep an eye on the countryside and speak in secret. The Baldknobbers fought against criminals and former Rebels, rarely distinguishing between the two; dozens were killed and hundreds more injured or driven from the area. The Southerners soon formed the antiBaldknobbers, and fighting between the two factions continued until a crackdown on both sides by Governor Marmaduke (ironically, a former Confederate cavalry raider.) In 1889 the Christian County court hanged three Baldknobbers for the murder of two of their enemies. It might be said that they were the last casualties of the American Civil War.

Jesse James used skills learned while serving under "Bloody Bill" Anderson to become an accomplished outlaw after the war, claiming – like many ex-Confederates – that he was driven to lawlessness by Federal persecution. He became a hero among former secessionists for his attacks on banks and trains, which were widely seen as owned by the same rich Northerners who had caused the war. In this reversed image he has three Colt Navy pistols and a typical, although undecorated, "guerrilla shirt." (LoC)

SELECT BIBLIOGRAPHY

Allen, Desmond Walls, ed., *Turnbo's Tales of the Ozarks: War and Guerrilla Stories* (Arkansas Research, 1989)

Bailey, Anne & Daniel Sutherland, eds., *Civil War Arkansas: Beyond Battles and Leaders* (University of Arkansas Press, Fayetteville, 2000)

Bailey, Joseph, *Confederate Guerrilla: The Civil War Memoir of Joseph Bailey* (University of Arkansas Press, Fayetteville, 2007)

Bright, Simeon Miller, "The McNeill Rangers: A Study in Confederate Guerrilla Warfare" in *West Virginia History* Vol. 12, No. 4 (July 1951), pp.338–387

Brownlee, Richard S., *Gray Ghosts of the Confederacy: Guerilla Warfare in the West, 1861–1865* (Louisiana State University Press, Baton Rouge, 1984)

Castel, Albert, "The Guerrilla War; 1861–1865" in *Civil War Times Illustrated*, October 1974

Derendinger, Elaine, Melba Fleck & and LaVaughn Miller, "Bill Anderson's Ambush of Captain Parks at Rawlings Lane, August 28, 1864" in *Stories of Howard County Missouri*, pp.121–122 (The South Howard County Historical Society, New Franklin, Missouri, 1999)

Downing, David, *A South Divided: Portraits of Dissent in the Confederacy*

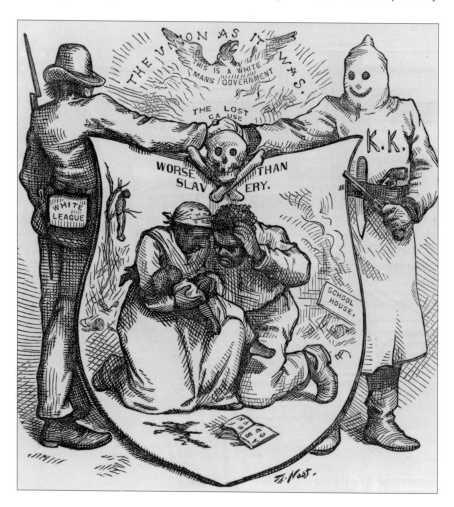

The Ku Klux Klan was a natural development of the South's failed guerrilla war against social and political change, and employed many of the same tactics of night raiding and targeting civilians. The relationship between Confederate veterans and the KKK is made clear in this sketch from the popular magazine *Harper's Weekly*. (LoC)

(Cumberland House, Nashville, 2007)

Hartman, Mary, & Joe Ingenthron, *Baldknobbers: Vigilantes on the Ozarks Frontier* (Pelican Publishing Company, Gretna, Louisiana, 1988)

Henry, Robert Selph, *"First With the Most" Forrest* (Broadfoot Publishing Company, Wilmington, North Carolina, 1987)

Huff, Leo, "Guerrillas, Jayhawkers and Bushwhackers in Northern Arkansas during the Civil War" in *Arkansas Historical Quarterly*, Vol. XXIV, No. 2, Summer 1965, pp.127–148

Hyde Jr., Samuel, "Bushwhacking and Barn Burning: Civil War Operations and the Florida Parishes' Tradition of Violence" in *Louisiana History*, Vol. XXXVI, No. 2 (Spring 1995), pp.171–186

Keller, Allan, *Morgan's Raid* (Bobbs-Merrill Company, Inc, New York 1961)

Kerby, Robert L, *Kirby Smith's Confederacy: The Trans-Mississippi South, 1863–1865* (University of Alabama Press, London, 1972)

Lathrop, Barnes, "The Lafourche District in 1862: Militia and Partisan Rangers" in *Louisiana History*, Vol. I, No. 3 (Summer 1960), pp.230–244

Leslie, Edward, *The Devil Knows How to Ride: The True Story of William Clarke Quantrill and His Confederate Raiders* (Da Capo Press, New York, 1996)

Longacre, Edward G, *Mounted Raids of the Civil War* (University of Nebraska Press, Lincoln, 1994)

Mackey, Robert R, *The Uncivil War: Irregular Warfare in the Upper South, 1861–1865* (University of Oklahoma Press, Norman, 2004)

McCorkle, John, *Three Years with Quantrill* (University of Oklahoma Press, Norman, 1992)

Michot, Stephen, "'War is Still Raging in This Part of the Country': Oath-Taking, Conscription, and the Guerrilla War in Louisiana's Lafourche Region" in *Louisiana History*, Vol. XXXVIII, No. 2 (Spring 1997), pp.157–184

Mudd, Joseph A, *With Porter in North Missouri* (Camp Pope Bookshop, Iowa City, 1992)

Mueller, Doris Land, *M. Jeff Thompson: Missouri's Swamp Fox of the Confederacy* (University of Missouri Press, Columbia, Missouri, 2007)

U.S. War Department, *The War of the Rebellion: A Compilation of the Official Records of the Union and Confederate Armies* (Government Printing Office, Washington, DC, 1888)

Watts, Hamp B., *The Babe of the Company: An Unfolded Leaf from the Forest of Never to-be-forgotten Years* (Democrat-Leader Press, Fayette, Missouri, 1913)

Yeatman, Ted, *Frank and Jesse James: The Story Behind the Legend* (Cumberland House, Nashville, 2000)

INDEX